THE ADVENTURES OF LILY THE SQUIRREL

Kevin Prochaska

INTRODUCTION

When our four children were very small, my wife Nancy and I would put them to bed at night in twin beds pushed together so they could sleep bundled up safe and warm, huddled next to each other. Each night before they went to sleep, I would tell them stories about Lily, a little white squirrel who lived in the Great Green Forest and of all the many exciting adventures she shared with her woodland friends. Lily's close friends included Einstein the Wise Old Owl, Mozart the Little Pink Dragon, Elvis the Toucan Bird, Robert the Moose, and Freddie the Indian. But were an owl, a dragon, a toucan bird, a moose, and an Indian the little squirrel's only friends? Heavens no! Add a Kangaroo from Kookaburra, an Elecan't, a monkey named Montezuma, and perhaps a few more characters, just for good measure, and Lily's stories become even more exciting!

I promised my now-grown children that I would one day write a book about Lily and her many friends and adventures, and I have finally done so. Hopefully, these stories will take them back to those childhood days when they sat on their beds giggling at the antics of Lily and her woodland friends.

Lily the Squirrel

Einstein the Wise Old Owl

Mozart the Little Pink Dragon

Elvis the Toucan Bird

Robert the Moose

Freddie the Indian

TABLE OF CONTENTS

CHAPTER 1

THE GREAT GREEN FOREST

Perhaps you've never ever heard of the Great Green Forest. I can understand why you haven't. It is kind of hidden away, just to try and keep it safe from prying eyes. But let me tell you about it then, and all the incredible and wonderful things happening within its calm and cleansing borders. The Great Green Forest is an absolutely fantastic and wondrous place to behold, as anyone who lives there or has ever visited there will tell you in the blink of a gnat's eye. It sits in the Southwest Corner of Nowhere, somewhere between the North and South Poles, and you must look for an extremely long time before you can find it. Perhaps it's for the best that this happy place will only be found by a lucky few and therefore will remain a secret. As a rule, privacy seems to keep things peaceful and less complicated in the long run.

The forest is vast and seems to go on forever, particularly for small woodland creatures built close to the ground, and, just like a child, too short to see very far ahead of their nose to begin with. The Great Green Forest is filled to the brim with thick, towering green trees and fat stubby bushes of seemingly endless varieties, some of which will never be found outside its borders. The forest seems to go on and on, stretching out forever in its emerald cloak, and wafting in the air are hundreds of tantalizing fragrances just waiting to be captured by the one lucky nose that happens to be passing by. The funny thing is, had that nose passed by a minute earlier, or even a second later, the tantalizing fragrance would have been something much different as puffs of winds coaxed more and more pleasant aromas into the air. And those millions of trees and bushes and vast expanses of grass snuggle closely against one another like pieces of a tight-fitting jigsaw puzzle, each piece separate from one another but easily recognizable as part of the whole grandeur. The grasses roll up and down the hills, a living, breathing roller coaster, calming into meadows flatter than the ice of a frozen lake. The trees are as green as Irish landscape across the broad expanse of the forest, but mixed with them are other not so green greens, and in other places are colors that are not green at all. Like some beautiful painting, all these colors seem to have been brushed together on one magnificent canvas by the hand of an unseen artist, all wise in his perception of beauty.

Below these towering trees lies a forest floor covered with leaves, pine needles, and pine cones, as well as smaller scrubs dispersed randomly upon the ground. Over the years, scattered branches ranging from the thinness of a pinky finger to the thickness of an elephant tusk have fallen from above, so numerous they give the appearance of an elephant's boneyard. Oftentimes one can find an entire grand elm or oak or even a pine tree that has crashed to the forest floor, still as majestic sprawled across the ground as when it was holding up the heavens. In certain spots the blackness of a perpetual night keeps the forest floor shaded, giving a refreshing relief to those bare feet lucky enough to tread upon the cool ground. The soil is composed of a loose organic mix, rich and moist, and more soil is constantly being made through nature's magical transformation called rotting. When the surface of the soil is scraped away, a wet earthy aroma delights the scraper's nostrils for one glorious moment and then returns down to its home in the soil. However, if touched, that same earthy aroma will cling to a foot or a hand or anything else touching it until a cleansing bath washes it away.

Below the rich soil on the forest floor lie hidden sediments in various colors of yellow, brown, black, and even red depending on where one happens to be. The Rogue River wiggles like a lazy snake through the entire length of the Great Green Forest, the water changing colors four times—from blue on entering to yellow to orange to red as the water passes through different colored soils along its banks. When heavy rains pour from the sky and the river rages in all its fury, the wriggling snake morphs into an angry serpent. The scene shifts as the four colors of the Rogue race along together, side by side, trying to mix but never quite able to do so. It is quite a sight to behold.

Right smack in the middle of the Great Green Forest sits a rather large mossy mound not quite round. Now a rather large mossy mound not quite round, as one would gather, is something almost never ever to be found. But allow me to now expound why it happens to be around. Legend has it that, long ago, this large mossy mound not quite round was built by the forest animals out of their love for the famous Indian warrior, Chief Root-En-Tatty, who once roamed the Great Green Forest many years (or moons, as the Chief would have said) ago. Chief Root-En-Tatty was a great Indian who ate only vegetables or fruits or nuts or berries or some combination thereof. The Chief was quite content to live in peace and harmony among all the creatures of the forest because he only ate vegetables or fruits or nuts or berries or some combination thereof, and never any animal, which made things very peaceful and convenient for both sides.

The only drawback in this arrangement appeared to be the Chief's loincloth. Because he loved the forest animals so much, his loincloth was, at first, made of large plant leaves sewn together. This simple act by the Chief allowed some poor rabbit or fox or deer to keep its fur and remain free to roam the forest not be draped across the Chief's body. Or, worse yet, have to run around furless, which would have a tendency to complicate things when the snow fell. Imagine the calamity of the poor fellow who saw a furless fox dart out of the bushes and run past him wearing nothing but pink skin jumping up and down with each passing step. Why, that by itself would be enough to stir up some pretty troublesome dreams.

Most warm days in the Great Green Forest, an observer would find the Chief contently sprawled in the middle of an enormous field of sun-drenched grass, far from the cooling shadows of the forest. Unfortunately, the vast canopy of trees hid much of the sky, so whenever it rained in the Great Green Forest, the storms broke suddenly, giving little warning of their approach. As the rain poured from the clouds, Chief Root-En-Tatty could be seen running for the cover of the trees, his hands firmly clutching his disintegrating loincloth while leaving a trail of wet leaves a blind beaver could follow, and turning his red face even redder than it normally was as the forest animals howled with laughter.

One particular night, under a beautiful blue sky dotted with millions of twinkling stars, Chief Root-En-Tatty gathered some wood to make his campfire, just as he did every other night of the year. After he stacked the wood at his campfire site, the Chief went into his teepee to get the two pieces of black flint he would scrape together to make the sparks that would fall upon the nest of dry leaves he piled in the middle of the wood and which would catch the sparks and start his fire.

But little did the Chief know two mischievous chipmunks named Roland and Artie had crept into his tepee earlier and stolen the two pieces of black flint, not to be mean, mind you, but just to play a trick on their big, lovable Indian friend. The mischievous chipmunks left in their place two pieces of black volcanic rock that looked, in the waning light, almost exactly like the flint the Chief used to start his fire. But, as some of you may know, just because a rock happens to come spewing from the top of a volcano doesn't mean it can make a spark like a flint rock can. Of course, the two rocks the mischievous Roland and Artie left in the Chief's tent couldn't flicker a single spark no matter how hard one tried to get them to do so. Chief Root-En-Tatty, unaware of the chipmunks' prank, began scraping the rocks gently together as he usually did every night but was quite surprised when not a single spark jumped out to fall on his pile of dried leaves.

Thinking the evening dew might have made them a bit damp, the Chief wiped them on his loincloth and scraped them a second time, this time a bit harder. But try as he might, no spark fell from the rocks to light his dry leaves. And the mischievous Roland and Artie, hiding behind a nearby rock, began to giggle, for the Indian was doing exactly what they thought he would do when they traded his spark-making flint for their non-sparking volcanic rocks. The Chief scraped harder and faster, and the little chipmunks started to giggle a little louder. The harder the Chief banged the rocks together, the more the chipmunks giggled, particularly because the Chief was making funny faces as he strained every fiber in his body to light his fire. The Chief scraped so hard he started to sweat and his fingers began to get tired. Several times his hands grew so sweaty he dropped the volcanic rocks and then had to search the ground to find them.

Finally, the Chief grew frustrated and stood up, huffing and puffing. He looked at the rocks in his hands and was so mad he flung them as hard as he could to the ground. It made no sense to him that a rock sparking one day would not spark the next. Unfortunately for the Chief, his feet were also on the ground, and both rocks he threw slammed into his tender little Indian toes. Now if the Chief thought his Indian toes were red before, they were even redder now. Getting one's toes slammed with volcanic rocks hurts something terribly, especially when you've unknowingly thrown them with all your might at your own feet. The Chief began hopping around his unlit campfire like a deranged rabbit whose ears had been stolen, and shouting things Indians, or anyone else, for that matter, should never be shouting out loud in any language. It looked like a war dance that had gotten way out of control.

The chipmunks could contain their giggles no longer and burst out laughing, rolling over and over near the rock behind which they hid. The Chief stopped hopping around when he heard this curious chipmunk laughter and crept over to see why anyone would be that happy when he was in so much pain, even though it was his own fault he was in so much agony. As he poked his head over the top of the rock and spotted the two laughing chipmunks, he also spotted the two pieces of flint they had taken from his tepee. He slowly reached his hand around the rock and reclaimed his flints and returned them to the safety of his tepee.

The Chief then brought out a bowl of honey and a sack of bird feathers he had collected from abandoned nests and other places in the forest and from which he made all sorts of beautiful trinkets. There were, indeed, many colors of feathers, for there were many different birds in the forest. As the chipmunks continued to roll around with laughter, he poured out some honey on the ground near them and then piled the feathers along the trail on which he was certain the chipmunks would have to use as they made their escape. He then returned to the fire and pretended to still be mad and hopped around some more, yelling and screaming at the top of his lungs, and the chipmunks rolled around in bigger circles, unable to control their laughter. As they rolled around in bigger and bigger circles, they soon rolled right into the puddle of honey but, in their laughter, failed to notice their fur was getting covered with a thick golden liquid.

Right about that time, Chief Root-En-Tatty jumped up from behind the rock and hollered at them with words like "you blankety-blank this" and "you blankety-blank that" as he furiously waved his nifty tomahawk back and forth over his head. Seeing the tomahawk, the chip munks jumped up too, not really understanding this "blankety-blank" language but assuming it was some ancient Indian dialect used to get an important point across. And though they were clueless as to what the Chief was saying, the purpose of the tomahawk was instantly clear to them. Roland and Artie beat a hasty retreat away from Chief Root-En-Tatty, heading pell-mell down the trail from which they had come just as fast as their little chipmunk legs could run. Of course, just as the crafty Chief had planned, the two chipmunks ran smack into the pile of colored feathers he had placed in the middle of the trail, and as you can guess, the two pranksters were immediately coated with many colors of feathers stuck to the honey in their fur.

Because Roland and Artie knew the Chief was hot on their tails, the chipmunks dared not linger to clean off the feathers but continued to run pell-mell along the path until they were well away from the Chief's campsite and heading to a clearing where they knew many of the forest creatures liked to hang out. As they burst into the clearing, they came upon dozens of forest animals and birds in the midst of a game of Pin the Tail on the Google Bird, a mythical bird that didn't exist but whose like-ness the animals made up so they could have something cool-looking to pin the tail on besides a boring donkey picture they used to have, now so full of pin holes it was more hole than paper. Just as Roland burst into the clearing, he ran right into a blindfolded possum named Edgar holding a red-feathered tail with a large tack sticking out of its end. The possum, feeling the feathers on Roland, assumed whatever was standing there was the Google Bird and, sensing opportunity, immediately jammed the sharp point of the tack as hard has he could deep into Roland's honey and feather-coated rear end.

Now if you thought Chief Root-En-Tatty hopped around after he threw rocks at his own toes, you should have seen Roland jump into the air after Edgar jabbed his rear with the sharp end of a tack. Roland sprang painfully into the air, a red-feathered tail hanging from his rear end. Artie burst into the clearing a moment later where he, too, experienced a similar fate from a blindfolded raccoon named Ringtail holding a blue-feathered tail who also assumed this feathery creature was the mythical Google bird into whose body he was supposed to thrust a pin. It was then Artie's turn to jump high into the air, yowling in pain from a blue-feathered tail embedded deeply into his rear end by Ringtail.

Hiding behind a large bush, Chief Root-En-Tatty watched the two chipmunks hopping painfully around inside a circle of woodland creatures, both chipmunks covered in colored feathers, with a red-feathered tail hanging from the rear end of Roland and a blue-feathered tail hanging from the rear end of Artie. The birds and animals laughed uncontrollably at the two failed pranksters who had quickly become the pranked, and from deep in the woods, Chief Root-En-Tatty howled with laughter so hard his leafy loincloth fell off. The Indian had to wrap it around himself and hold it in place with one hand as he returned to his tepee to find a piece of rope to keep it in place.

For several weeks afterward, the animals of the forest made fun of Roland and Artie and even went as far as to report sightings of something quite new to the forest—an animal apparently part bird and part chipmunk, something they called a Rainbow-Colored-Feather-Rear-End-Sticking-Chipmunk Squawker running amuck somewhere in the deepest recesses of the Great Green Forest.

CHAPTER 2

A LARGE MOSSY MOUND
NOT QUITE ROUND

But, getting back to the rather large mossy mound not quite round and almost never to be found, of which I told you earlier I would expound. After Chief Root-En-Tatty recovered his flint rocks and chased away the mischievous chipmunks, he returned to his campsite and soaked his battered toes in the cool flowing waters of the Rogue River to relieve his body of the throbbing pain he'd given himself by flinging rocks at his own feet. He did finally manage to scrape his two flints together, and brilliant sparks flew into a nest of dry leaves, bringing his campfire to life while clearing the surrounding area of that pesky darkness.

As the fire grew bright, the Chief began cutting up and cooking the fresh wild mushrooms he spent all afternoon gathering in the Great Green Forest. He cooked them in a delicious white dandelion sauce and had to admit to himself this concoction he'd invented tasted pretty darn good. The Chief cooked a second batch and thought those tasted even better than the pretty darn good ones he'd just had, concluding rightfully it was because he'd used twice as much white dandelion sauce in the second batch as he had in the first. The good Chief cut up and cooked the remaining mushrooms in an absolute ocean of white dandelion sauce and ate every single bit of them, even a hot dab that had fallen on one of his swollen toes whose numbness couldn't feel the heat of the sauce anyway. He licked his lips gleefully, concluding the third batch had, for sure, been the best tasting of the three. His toes even seemed to be feeling better! Perhaps, the Chief thought, he had stumbled upon a secret remedy for relieving swollen toes! Maybe he could sell the recipe and get rich!

All the exciting events of the day and all the food he had eaten finally caught up with Chief Root-En-Tatty, and as you can imagine, he grew very tired as he sat around his warm campfire. The flames seemed to dance before his eyes, and the heat radiating from the fire made his eyes very heavy. He finally fell asleep on his blanket right next to the soothing fire and soon snored away like a sleeping elephant whose trunk was plugged up with about five pounds of nasty green boogers.

Now we'll never know whether it was the delicious mushrooms or the white dandelion sauce that caused the Chief's strange dreams, or perhaps even a combination of the two. But we do know the Chief was quite a dreamer—a world-class dreamer, as a matter of fact. When he was extremely deep into his dreams, his sleeping brain would instruct his slumbering body to act out whatever it was he happened to be dreaming, and the gyrations of his body as he slept were indeed something quite spectacular to behold.

Woodland animals would often gather just beyond the faint light of the campfire to watch the Chief's antics as he slept. Some nights the Chief would lie on his back and stick his hands and legs in the air and run as fast as he could, and all the animals and birds would howl with laughter and wonder what it was their Indian friend was chasing. Sometimes the Chief would swing his arms back and forth over his head and then down past his sides as he kicked his legs, and the animals and birds would laugh uncontrollably because they knew the Indian dreamed he was a huge bear swimming after a yummy fish in some distant yet invisible lake. And sometimes the animals would watch as the Chief pulled back his bow, sending an arrow toward some unknown target, and then grin with immense satisfaction as the arrow found its mark. But the Chief was funniest when he dreamed even weirder things, and all the animals and birds would roll on the ground with laughter as the Chief would act like some grizzly trying to climb a tree that wasn't there or turn his face skyward and howl like a lonely wolf crying to the moon.

Now if the truth were to be known, it was the Chief's dream antics that were the reason he never had any trouble finding mushrooms or white dandelion sauce to cook them in. The animals loved to watch the Chief dream, for it amused them to no end, and they planted lots of mushrooms very close to his teepee so the Chief wouldn't have to venture very far from his camp to find them. Sometimes the woodland animals picked full-grown mushrooms from faraway locations and carried them to the Chief's campsite and stuck them back into the soft ground so the Chief wouldn't have to waste a lot of time searching for them. They knew he could get right to the task of cooking them in white dandelion sauce, and the animals anxiously waiting for the Chief to go to sleep would be assured of yet another night of hilarious entertainment as he gyrated in his dreams.

On this particular night, however, none of the forest animals came to watch the Chief dreaming because they were all still in the clearing, laughing at the two chipmunks, Roland and Artie, hopping around in colored feathers with Google Bird tails sticking out of their rear ends. It would be just too much fun for any creature to handle, for they had all heard the story of Felipe the Raccoon who once laughed so hard he fractured his funny bone and thus didn't dare laugh for a whole year. And there are fewer things more pathetic than watching a raccoon trying to mime his laugh—that just doesn't work well when one has arms that short.

While the Chief slept unobserved this night, he dreamed he was a world-class cliff diver plunging into the depths of the great Niagara Falls. The Chief had heard a great deal about the gigantic waterfalls but had never been there, though traveling to see it one day was indeed high on his bucket list. With no one around to see him, the sleeping Chief rose from his slumber and commenced sleepwalking toward the only waterfalls nearby, the Do Drop Falls on the Rogue River. In his dream he was a world-class diver standing at the edge of the waterfall. With his eyes closed, he lifted his hands into the air and smiled confidently. With a mighty effort, he plunged like the blade of a sharp knife into the tor-rential waters below the Do Drop Falls. Unfortunately, the water where the Chief chose to dive was neither great nor deep.

The forest animals found poor Chief Root-En-Tatty the next morn-ing on the banks of the Rogue River, and though not among the living anymore, the gentle Chief had an extremely large smile upon his sleep-ing face as well as a good-sized bump on his forehead. The Great Green Forest family had lost their beloved Chief and world-class dreamer, and though all the creatures of the woodlands were quite sad at his passing, they took comfort in knowing their friend was at least squeaky clean when he arrived at the Happy Hunting Grounds he always talked about.

Now, getting back once more to the rather large mossy mound not quite round and almost never to be found, of which I promised you twice already I would expound. I will do so right now. The animals deeply loved and held in high regard Chief Root-En-Tatty, and they carried him on willow branches to a place in the forest near his teepee, a shallow depression the Chief had loved because it was his favorite mushroom hunting spot. It was the spot where the friendly animals planted these delectable delights in abundance so the Chief might easily find them. Here they lovingly laid their friend to rest in the shallow depression on the forest floor, piling leaves, branches, and other forest things around him like a warm blanket after tenderly placing on his body little gifts of painted oak leaves, long necklaces of acorns, trinkets made of feathers tied with sticks, and other such artwork for the Chief to wear or play with as he romped happily in the Happy Hunting Grounds and thus possess tokens of remembrance from all his woodland friends as he did so. On each of his closed eyes, the animals laid one of his precious flint rocks so their friend would always have a means to keep himself warm on his journey.

The Chief was soon covered with hundreds of presents and the depression filled to the brim and grew up to form a mound. To protect the sacred spot from both the weather and thieves, the forest creatures formed a long line from the banks of the Rogue River to the Chief's resting place, covering the Indian and his trinkets with rich mud from the river bottom. Soon the task was done, and the good Chief was safe from all that might harm him, under the mound not quite round and almost never to be found his friends had lovingly built. The funny thing is, even now, if you look at the mound a certain way when the sun shines on it just right, it does look like an Indian Chief lying on his back and staring up in wonder at an endless sky, maybe still adding to that bucket list he was making. Perhaps that is why the mound is not quite round.

CHAPTER 3

SCAT BURIES AN OAK SEED

The mound not quite round rested in the afternoon shadows of a huge weeping willow tree also seeming to mourn the Chief's passing. For a time, the mound was watered every day by the shedding of the willow's soft tears upon the warm earth covering the Chief's resting place. The combination of the willow's tears falling upon the rich river mud and the many hours spent under the willow's protective shade very quickly caused a thick bed of green moss to grow over the mound. And one day, a few weeks later, a squirrel named Scat, not from the Great Green Forest, happened along, carrying in his mouth an acorn, not an uncommon sight to behold in the woods. It is a well-known fact that squirrels always have to wander to and fro carrying something in their mouth or at least have to be digging around somewhere to find something to put in their mouth. Squirrels, as you probably know, have these big front teeth they like to show off to everyone who throws a glance their way, and carrying around nuts in their mouth half the day is an excellent way to do this without appearing as if they intentionally mean to be showing off that gleaming white fencerow usually hidden behind their lips.

As squirrels would be, Scat was no different, maintaining he just *had* to bury *something* at least once on this day or risk the chance of being made fun of or called lazy by other squirrels competing with each other for recognition. Since the sky was growing dark and he had failed to bury anything all day, Scat found himself standing on the very top of Chief Root-En-Tatty's mound, having not the slightest idea someone so noble was buried in the warm soil just below where he stood. His jaws were tired from having his mouth open carrying the big acorn since high noon because, in his joy at wandering and discovering new things, he had, amazingly, forgot for a while he even carried anything at all in his mouth. But now he concluded this would be just the perfect time to get rid of his burden so he could once again move his jaws back and forth and get some relief for his stretched cheek muscles while also halting the stream of gooey saliva drooling from his mouth and onto his chin. Scat did just that. Standing on the highest point on the mound, the squirrel dug furiously through the thick moss and into the rich river mud to bury the acorn. When the hole was deep enough, Scat dropped the acorn from his mouth and into the hole, quickly filling it by scraping the river mud back into place with his nose and pushing the moss over it. As Scat finished his task, he scanned around in every direction to see if any other animals were spying on him. Scat's keen eyes roamed the surrounding ground, bushes, and the high trees above until the squirrel was satisfied no one watched him, content his acorn would remain hidden.

But in truth, if Scat had known the peculiar habits of squirrels, he needn't have worried at all. You see, although squirrels all over the world bury jillions and jillions of nuts of every kind every year, they are very jealous of their hiding places and don't want other squirrels to find them and dig them up. That seems to work pretty well because in the entire vast history of squirrels, not one of these squirrels that buried a nut ever returned to dig it back up, and no other squirrels ever found it either. That *includes* George Washington's cherry tree—yes, a squirrel did, indeed, bury that seed, albeit with the plump cherry meat still around the seed; no offense meant to the farsighted furry tail flicker that did it. Squirrels are born a tad addle-brained and can't remember what they did yesterday, let alone where they buried a nut the day before or that they even buried a nut at all. But there are those who say it's a good thing squirrels can't remember very well. Those little furry animals with the bad memories planted jillions and jillions of trees for everyone to enjoy, unknowingly becoming the unheralded Johnny Appleseeds of the animal kingdom and much more diverse in their selection than Johnny ever dreamed of being.

Scat buried the acorn at exactly the right time. That very night, great storm clouds covered the Great Green Forest, soaking the mound not quite round with cleansing rainwater. The rainwater poured through the loosened soil under which Scat had buried the oak seed, swelling the acorn until its shell cracked. The little acorn seed tucked inside the shell now began to stir. A short while later, the tiny head of an oak tree sprouted from the mossy mound and delicate twiggy fingers reached up toward the sun. The sun shone brilliant rays upon the little tree, favoring it with all the sunshine the little oak would ever need to grow strong and tall. As the little tree shot upward, its trunk grew taller and its branches reached out like huge arms with green hands. When the wind blew, it looked as if the green fingers of the hands were reaching out, trying to capture passing clouds and wring out their water like a sponge to grow the tree even larger.

The years passed quickly and the tree grew taller and thicker to eventually tower over the weeping willow under whose shadows it used to hide. Its thick roots plunged deeper and deeper into the depths of the not-quite-round mound. One day the roots bumped against a strange object buried in the ground beneath it—something quite hard. The strange object the root discovered was Chief Root-En-Tatty, and the gentle Chief's body rested exactly as it had been when the forest animals tenderly placed him there so many years before—with one exception. The kindly Indian's body had changed in a way no one could have imagined. All the mud the forest creatures had covered the Chief with had absorbed into the Indian's body, and it turned to solid stone!

Over the course of time, the roots of the oak curled around the good Chief as they grew downward, and soon the stone body and all the gifts the forest animals lovingly placed next to it were entirely encased and protected as if by a sturdy wooden suit of armor. It's kind of funny when you think about it—a Chief with "Root" in his name surrounded and protected by roots. The tree continued to grow, becoming even taller and thicker, with large branches stretching out in all directions from its massive trunk. It grew to a height of over 150 feet tall and eventually stood higher than any tree in the Great Green Forest. The mound was no longer easy to see, dwarfed by the oak tree in its center and disturbed by the movement of gigantic roots below. The Big Oak, as it was now known by the forest animals, could be seen from anywhere in the forest, which made it extremely convenient for any creature to find their bearings. If one found oneself lost, the Big Oak looming over the forest would be the guide to see them safely on their way.

One cold winter, the Big Oak was covered with an unusually thick blanket of snow, the biggest snowfall the forest had ever seen. Part of a small branch of the tree broke off and crashed to the ground, leaving an ugly gash in the main trunk just above the tree's thickest and lowest branch. As spring came and the weather grew warm, the big gash in the tree began to bleed, and the tree was in danger of dying as all its tree liquid began flowing down its magnificent trunk in a thick waterfall of what looked like brown syrup. Fortunately, trees can repair themselves when they're hurt, and the mighty oak began to plug the hole where the tree was bleeding. The oak surrounded the gash with a crust of gnarly bark, like a thick scab over a wound. The crusty scab did a remarkable job of slowing down the flow, and soon there was nothing left but a dark round hole surrounded by a thick ring of bark sticking out from the main trunk. When the gash eventually dried, the knothole stopped growing as well, leaving a round hole in the middle, exactly where a hole in a knothole is generally supposed to be located.

What does one do with a knothole? What use could a knothole possibly have? It's way up in the air, just above the thickest and lowest branch of the Big Oak. But, it is a hole, and it's a pretty tough job to try and pry it out of the tree because once you do, the only thing you'd get out of this experiment is to create a bigger hole. Then you'd have one little hole in your hand and a second, bigger one in the spot where you just pried out the little one. That won't work very well, and you'd have only created a second problem, as you can plainly see. And if you pried the second hole out, you'd get a third hole, and if you pried the third hole out, well, you can see this hole-prying ordeal might go on until you ran out of tree. So, back to the question—what does one do with a knothole? It's still there and it's not going to go away.

But one can still do a lot with something that has nothing in it because you can always fit something into nothing, although not as easily as you can fit nothing into something. Doing something with nothing is what some forest creatures would call a *thinkory*, and most *thinkory* things must be acted upon immediately before someone else figures out their well thought-out *thinkory* wouldn't ever work. Then things wouldn't be good for either side and therefore should never be tried. But, making something from nothing, in the end, is exactly what happened to the little hole in the tree.

CHAPTER 4

BEHIND AN ITTY-BITTY DOOR

Just inside the knothole that saved the Big Oak long ago now sits an itty-bitty brown door made of several very narrow vertical boards. The door is rounded at the top and hangs on shiny brass hinges with a shiny brass lock on the left side. Slightly above the shiny brass lock, a tan doorknob made from an extremely large pecan nut juts out, and every first-time visitor always remarks how clever an idea it was to use an oblong nut instead of an ordinary run-of-the-mill round nut for a doorknob. For anyone can have a round doorknob, they tell me, but not everyone has a doorknob that's oblong. Besides, a round knob can slip away from a wet paw, but an oblong knob won't. For some reason, that's pretty cool.

Now right behind the itty-bitty brown door with a doorknob made from an extremely large pecan nut lives a funny little squirrel. She is quite an interesting squirrel because in a forest where all the other squirrels have magnificent furs of brown or gray, or an occasional red, she is the only squirrel whose fur is pure white. Her fur, as a matter of fact, is as white as newly fallen snow. What is amazing is that she is the only white-furred squirrel in the Great Green Forest and the only one who has ever been. And as further wonders reveal, she was not born with this white fur—not at all—and I will tell you how this came about.

You see this particular squirrel was born at an odd time of year. Usually, squirrel babies are born in spring, but not this one. She arrived in late winter, born smack between the middle of the peaking of a half-moon whose left side was hidden in the shadows of an eerie blue night sky and at the rising of a bright orange new day sun. Our new arrival came into the world right about the time a fierce, raging blizzard swept through the Great Green Forest. The storm drove a howling gust of wind through the oversized brass lock on the itty-bitty door protecting her as she slumbered in her tiny nest of oak leaves. The fierce wind failed to wake the newborn squirrel even as a swirling mist in the shape of a tiny tornado burst into the room. Its little funnel was filled to the brim with pure white sparkling snow. The white funnel danced around the oak leaf nest as if wondering what mayhem it could provoke and then went about completing the mischief it had pondered. The white tornado shook once, then twice, and then thrice, dancing around the little nest and dropping upon the sleeping baby's brown fur a gentle dusting of white sparkling snow. Of course, as a newborn baby, the brown squirrel was unaware of these events and continued to sleep soundly through all the noise and havoc going on around her.

Since she was barely a week old, the squirrel had no knowledge of the world yet and, therefore, no memories. She had yet to have one dream, for dreams require memories of things that had been or might have been, and her sleep was deep and undisturbed as the snow fell gently upon her still body. The baby squirrel's brown fur was totally covered with fresh white snow which her little body gratefully absorbed, transforming the thick brown fur into the whitest white you have ever seen. The tiny tornado, its mischief complete, swirled silently out the door. The snow remained upon her when the wind died and the bright orange new day sun peeked its head over the snow-covered Great Green Forest. As the snow melted away, the fur remained white, and no trace—not one hair—of her formerly brown coat could be found. Even her whiskers were white.

When the young squirrel's parents returned home, they found only a pile of white in the nest and became understandably quite alarmed their young one was missing. But as they gazed down upon that white mound in the nest, a blue eye suddenly opened and twinkled up at them. They knew then that their child was still in the nest, but now sporting a coat of fur as white as the snow outside. Not understanding quite what happened, they never paused for a moment to dwell upon the reason why this remarkable event ever took place. They merely accepted it as something that now was and that was that. Acceptance was just a way of life in the animal kingdom and in the Great Green Forest as well. They called their new baby squirrel Lily and went about the extremely important business of raising their offspring properly.

A few days later, Lily ventured outside and sat on the snow-covered great big branch just below the itty-bitty door. Excited by the new world she found, she began chirping down to all those strange animals passing by below the tree, for she had never seen anything like them. Since her white fur was invisible against the snowy branches, she immediately frightened all those poor creatures happening by. For some time afterward, they avoided the great big tree with the great big branch with the itty-bitty door because they all thought an invisible spirit who could see and speak to them, but was most likely too hideous to show itself, now haunted the very soul of the towering Big Oak. Some rumors even spread that the great Chief Root-En-Tatty might have come back to haunt the tree, perhaps angry because no one bothered to wake him up before he dove into the waters of the Rogue River and bonked his head on the rocks and then ended up petrified in stone and was now held prisoner in a mass of sturdy roots beneath the Big Oak.

But, eventually, Lily grew tired of animals running away from her and having no one to play with or talk to because all of them were too afraid to approach her tree. For a short time, Lily wore an orange glow stick around her neck, so brilliant it could be seen easily from far away. When the woodland animals could see the glowing stick and speak to the white squirrel wearing it, they got to know what a friendly animal she was and they stopped running away, and the rumors of an invisible spirit haunting the tree gradually went away. Losing their fear of the Big Oak proved to be a great thing for Lily because all the animals of the forest were now her friends and accepted the squirrel for what she was, a snow-white squirrel and not a plain ordinary vanilla run-of-the-mill brown squirrel, or even one of those common gray ones rumored to exist in forests far away.

CHAPTER 5

THE FOREST FRIENDS

Lily now lives by herself in the hole behind the itty-bitty door above the large branch of the Big Oak. One of her favorite pastimes is playing hide-and-seek with all the forest friends, although the poor little thing is not very good at it. But it's not Lily's fault really because it's pretty hard to hide a pure white fur coat in a forest of dark greenery. She's always one of the first animals to be spotted no matter how hard she tries to hide among the lush foliage covering the forest roof high above the mossy floor and green meadows of the Great Green Forest. Lily's fur is very soft and very fluffy, and every fine hair catches the morning rays and sparkles brightly in the sunlight. When Lily laughs, which she does quite frequently, her big blue eyes twinkle like little stars and the long whiskers of her nose twitch as if caught in the quivering shake of a laughing earthquake. Now I bet you didn't know squirrels could laugh, did you? Well, they can. You will learn many more things later you didn't know about squirrels. So stick around!

Lily has met scads and scads of friends in the Great Green Forest, each quite unique in their own right. Perhaps the greatest source of knowledge and wisdom within the forest is Einstein the Wise Old Owl. Einstein is a large oval-shaped bird with various colors of white, yellow, and shades of brown mixed in his magnificent array of feathers. Einstein has a tendency to act a bit proper and stodgy, like some old English aristocratic gentleman, and one would think at first he's quite gruff, but he's as gentle as a lamb. Einstein likes to ponder about matters, gathering his thoughts in a logical and orderly progression before giving his opinion on things. A keen pair of eyes comes in real handy when danger occasionally lurks about, and Einstein has been blessed with great vision. The sharp-eyed owl can spot things happening at distances that no other woodland creature can see. If Einstein says he can see a field mouse under a bush half a mile away, you'd better believe him because what he's saying is true.

If some bird or animal in the forest has a question or concern, they come to Einstein with it first, and usually they will go away satisfied with an answer the owl has, in his wisdom, provided that is both correct and logically explained. But to be fair, the owl cannot answer certain questions, such as the number of knotholes in the forest or the direction of the solar wind on Pluto or the length of the part of the Great Wall of China never built, at least not without having to conceal a sly smirk.

Mozart the Little Pink Dragon is a funny little character, mainly because he is the only dragon in known history that has ever lived in the Great Green Forest. He is very small, barely the size of a good-sized mushroom. By the way, Mozart *is* pink as well, as if his name didn't already imply that, and upon his back sits a splatter of black polka dots Mother Nature apparently threw in as an added bonus when she issued Mozart his skin. Also on his back is a row of what looks like little green teeth jutting out from the top of his head and extending along his body to the tip of his little dragon tail. From high on his back sprouts a pair of tiny pink wings covered with pink scales, one on either side of the row of green teeth riding down his back. Sometimes when Mozart opens his mouth a pink flame emerges, but fortunately for those around him, his flame never comes out very far beyond his tongue, which makes it convenient on those occasions when he coughs or sneezes and those pink flames burst forth. Some forest animals have wondered if Mozart could even muster a flame decent enough to roast a marshmallow. The poor dragon once sucked dandelion fuzz up his nose, and the ensuing sneeze burned the eyebrows clean off poor Bruno the Badger who was merely trying to sun himself on a rock near Paula's Pond. Mozart can never spit, even when he tries, because his spit is lost in pink flames and therefore comes dancing out of the little dragon's mouth as a wiggly cloud of pink steam.

The great thing about Mozart is he's very friendly and quite musical as well. Mozart has the most unique musical instrument, or, more accurately, an array of musical instruments, I should say. His musical menagerie consists of a wide variety of mushrooms with thick, stout stems topped by hardy caps tough as leather. The booming of drums and rapping of bongos resound through the forest whenever the dragon takes a notion to bang on them. Mozart's huge advantage over all other drummers in the animal world, or human world for that matter, is the dragon can bang on the mushroom drums not only with his tiny front claws but also by whipping his dragon tail around to pound on them. There is nowhere in the world one can go to find a three-armed drummer, but Mozart comes close. Sometimes the dragon whips the teeth of his tail across the tops of the mushrooms to make the music of a harp with the smaller teeth or a cello sound when he scrapes the larger teeth.

Mozart is a sight to behold when he gets into a rhythm on his drums, banging out all sorts of lively tunes. There isn't a melody he can't drum out when he sets his claws and tail to it. What's even more amazing is that he never uses a music sheet to read. That right there is quite a remarkable feat in itself. Mozart calls his drum set the Magical Mushroom Patch, and it is extremely magical because of one very unique feature that has nothing to do with music. Each night the Magical Mushroom Patch moves by some mysterious force from one place in the Great Green Forest to another, but somehow Mozart not only always knows where the Magical Mushroom Patch will appear the following morning but also what time it will arrive at its new location. Mozart doesn't know why this happens, but as we have already mentioned, acceptance is just a way of life in the animal kingdom and in the Great Green Forest as well.

The sight of the little pink dragon banging away on his drums in the light of a full moon while being surrounded by all the forest animals is indeed a vision to behold. In the light of the moon, the caps of the mushrooms twinkle like stars in the sky, and when Mozart bangs on the caps, the twinkling lights bounce into the air like fairy dust and then fall back down like the tail of a shooting star to land exactly where they were before they jumped up. When the Magical Mushroom Patch appears next to Paula's Pond, and Mozart bangs away on his drums, fish like Carl the Carp will often stick their heads out above the calm surface of the pond and swish back and forth to the beat. It is quite a sight to behold on a warm summer's night to see hundreds of fish poking their heads out of the water as the sound of drums thunders along the surface of the water. A pair of green bullfrogs named Finnegan and Finagle will incvitably hop from thc pond and leap upon a large rock on the shore, their skinny frog legs moving in time to the rhythm of the beat.

Elvis the Toucan Bird lives in the Great Green Forest although how he got there is a bit of a mystery. You see, toucan birds are supposed to live in the rainforest of South America, and the Great Green Forest is certainly neither in South America nor in a rainforest. Rumor has it Elvis came from South America as a baby bird and the cage Elvis was traveling in fell from an old man's cart one day as he happened to roll close by the edge of the forest. The cage apparently bounced to the ground and burst open, springing little Elvis free. Elvis just wandered into the woods and was found by some sympathetic woodland creatures who helped raise the little toucan to become an upstanding citizen of the forest. Elvis has adapted to the Great Green Forest quite nicely and has never known any other home.

Elvis is indeed the most colorful bird in the forest. His entire body is covered with shiny black feathers, with the exception of a large patch of yellow feathers right beneath his beak. The yellow feathers make Elvis look like he's wearing a baby bib, and the poor fellow is often teased about being a sloppy eater because Mother Nature, in her wisdom, fitted him with a feather bib even before he was born. Unusual for a toucan, Elvis sports a shock of shiny and greasy-looking black hair on the top of his head, the hair curling down over his not prominent forehead to rest just over his left eye. When a sudden gust of wind happens by, the hair swings back and forth across his eyes like the pendulum of a clock and the poor bird must either turn away from the wind or sweep the shock back into place with a flip of his head.

But the first thing you notice about Elvis is his enormous yellow beak jutting way out in front of his head. The top of this long appendage curves downward, and the whole beak looks like an enormous banana sticking out and makes the bird's head appear to be quite small when, in fact, it's not. Sometimes other forest creatures yell out, "Hey, Banana Nose!" when Elvis comes by, not to be mean, mind you, but just to poke fun at him. Elvis' feet are unusual too because they're robin egg blue, and if you touched them, they feel like soft leather freshly oiled. Elvis likes to tell other forest creatures meeting him for the first time that he's wearing blue suede shoes. That always gets a laugh when he says it. Elvis has quite a vivid imagination and is always saying interesting things. One such thing he says when he spots two young forest creatures walking paw in paw along a lonely path is they have a "hunk of burning love" which is kind of a weird way of saying they like each other a lot. But that's just Elvis, and every forest creature is well aware sooner or later the colorful toucan will come up with something even a little weirder to say, and maybe about them.

Robert the Moose is the largest animal in the forest and has a coat of dark scraggily brown fur, as if each hair wanted to go in a different direction but was frozen in mid-flight. The scraggily fur is draped over the moose's gangly body, and it looks as if he's starving when, indeed, he eats very well with all the ample and various kinds of food available in the forest. His head is always drooping to the ground, weighed down by a pair of enormous antlers resting on top of his head like two trees sprouting from his skull and growing out in opposite directions. There are those who wonder if little branches were to grow out from those antlers just what kind of leaves or fruits or nuts might end up hanging there, ripening in the sun.

Robert's drooping head makes him appear like he's sad and forlorn when, in actuality, he's quite a happy-go-lucky fellow. Robert's vice, or virtue if you ask him, is that he's just not very ambitious. The gangly moose can often be spotted in the warmth of the summer sun and sleeping soundly as the shadows of passing clouds roll over his body and rile his fur.

Robert can sometimes be observed with his antlers full of strange-colored ornaments hanging from a thin rope stretching from one antler to the other. You see, the forest animals have taken to using Robert's antlers as a place to hang their laundry, and it is quite a sight to watch all the colors of cloth swinging in the breeze between Robert's ears as the moose dozes contently beneath them. Some mischievous mice or chipmunks or some other kinds of prankster have been known to sneak other items onto the antlers while Robert snores away. The moose has ambled down to Paula's Pond many times following his nap to discover items like pine cone snowmen or twiggy birds or large leaves impaled on the tip of an antler while he slept, and the only way to get rid of at this hindrance is for Robert to plunge into the cool waters of the pond to separate his antlers from the prankster's artwork.

Robert often forgets how big his antlers are, and sometimes the forest erupts with the cry of, "Oh, blast it all!" echoing through the trees as, "Oh, blast it all… oh, blast it all… oh, blast it all," becoming quieter with distance and weakening to a whisper before disappearing into the thin forest air. When this happens, all the animals of the forest know Robert has banged into something or caught his antlers on a bush or some other hindrances and the moose is not very happy about it. But the big moose never stays distraught for very long. It's just not in Robert's nature to be sad.

Freddie the Indian lives in the Great Green Forest as well and is the only human who lives there. He is quite tall but skinny, except for his belly which bulges out a bit with an outie belly button poking out from his stomach sort of like a small tongue jutting out of a mouth. Freddie's long black hair shines as if it's been perpetually greased and dangles down to his shoulders most days, except when Freddie dresses up for special occasions. When the gentle Indian goes all out and braids his hair, he weaves into the braids fun things like feathers or hairpieces he has fashioned from leather or wood. On special occasions Freddie will don a richly ornate Indian bonnet. The headdress rises high over his head and then drops over his back and follows his legs until stopping just before touching the ground. The bonnet is beautifully arrayed with white feathers arranged in rows like a fence, and midway down each feather are two leather straps, one red and one blue, weaving parallel around each feather to keep them fastened securely in the bonnet.

Unlike his distant ancestor Chief Root-En-Tatty, wearer of his trademark leafy loincloth, Freddie the Indian wears a loincloth made of things other than leaves. He did attempt wearing leaves for a while, but things got a little embarrassing when autumn arrived and the leaves began to fall, just as they did with Chief Root-En-Tatty, so Freddie had to change up his wardrobe to more appropriate garb. Freddie now designs his loincloths from many materials, depending on the season or occasion, and he is very innovative, choosing fur, leather, cloth, and even tree barks, vines, or, on rare occasion, leaves. It is quite surprising to see what kind of loincloth the inventive Indian will be wearing when he emerges from his tepee. But whatever loincloth adorns the Indian's beanpole frame, it always appears the fragile garment is only about half a breeze away from being whisked into the air.

Freddie's teepee is located right next to Paula's Pond, and every night the flame from his campfire reflects off the water, lighting up the woods for quite a distance. Over the campfire a visitor will sometimes be treated to one of Freddie's Famous Pemmican Pies, made from all sorts of forest delights. No two pies ever taste the same because the delicacies Freddie puts in them change from day to day. This inconsistency in recipes is most likely due to the Indian's not-so-razor-sharp memory rather than innovation on his part. In the winter, Freddie tops his Pemmican Pie with a hearty helping of fresh cold snow that melts on the warm pie and trickles down into the crust to make the delicacy even juicier. Freddie is indeed a friend of the forest, and all the animals adore this tall gentle giant.

Lily, as you will soon see, has scads of other friends in the Great Green Forest, and we will meet many of them as we journey along the way. Occasionally, other strange and wonderful creatures wander into the Great Green Forest, and they bring fun and excitement with them as well. Lily and her many friends have lots of adventures, and even as I speak, Lily is right out in the Great Green Forest, smack dab in the middle of one of her great adventures. But before we get to Lily's adventures, let me tell you a quick story about a pond.

CHAPTER 6

PAULA'S POND

Mother Nature is about the only one who knows Paula's Pond wasn't always in the Great Green Forest. That's pretty odd, wouldn't you say? In fact, to be truthful, Paula's Pond didn't start out as water at all. Paula's Pond, believe it or not, started out as a very large chunk of blue ice trapped deep within the belly of a monstrous glacier hundreds of miles from the Great Green Forest. Paula's Pond would have been quite content to remain as just one of those thousands of pieces of ice squeezed together, but for the fact, nature has a way of shaking things up just about the time the world gets comfortable with what is. That is exactly what happened to Paula's Pond.

For a couple of hundred years, ice sheets peeled off from this monstrous glacier and fell into the ocean hundreds of feet below until the ice destined to become Paula's Pond hung perilously from the side of the glacier, content to cling there and just kind of watch the clouds roll by. The pond could feel the glacier jerk every now and then but did not understand why something so big would feel the need to move at all. After all, how could a patch of unthinking frozen ice realize the glacier upon which it rode was getting bigger, adding on new snow and ice every season, and the weight of all the new snow and ice was causing the glacier to move, very slowly, mind you, but definitely crawling forward. Not only did all that ice move but also did everything else trapped

33

in the snow before it turned to ice and joined the glacier. Tons and tons of rocks of all sorts and sizes were trapped in the ice, and from a distance the face of the glacier looked like a big blue-and-white cookie with lots and lots of raisins and chocolate chips added for flavor. Of course, the ice captured other things like trees and bushes and carried them right along as well. But sometimes other things, quite surprising things, were trapped in the ice as well.

Everything appeared to be just peachy within the massive ice sheet, all part of the natural order until one windy day something abruptly happened to change things. Paula's Pond was hanging out on the ice cliff of the glacier one morning when the air was suddenly pierced by a thunderous boom from somewhere deep in the heart of the ice. The boom rolled up and down the face of all the ice cliffs for miles around, and it was as if the whole world shook. The boom was immediately followed by a crackling noise, as if a million pieces of glass had just shattered on a cement floor. Paula's Pond felt a tremendous shudder, like the force of an earthquake. A gigantic wedge of blue ice became weightless and abruptly plunged straight down. Paula's Pond was part of a huge piece of the glacier that had broken off the main ice sheet, and this huge block of ice hurled toward the vast surface of an ocean 500 feet below. The gigantic expanse of ice plopped with a tremendous splash as it hit the water. The ice, over 400 feet high, hit the ocean with such speed the entire block sank below the waves for a split second before bobbing up like a gigantic whale breaching the surface.

The titanic piece of ice became an iceberg in itself, floating aimlessly in the cold sea. Its plunge into the water created gigantic waves rushing across the face of the sea, speeding away from the iceberg. Some of the waves rammed against other glaciers and other icebergs, and some more ambitious waves continued on for several hundred miles, crashing into distant islands to launch herds of walruses or flocks of penguins off the rocks and into the water. The waves traveled out into the vastness of the ocean where they finally ran out of energy and left no telltale signs they had ever been there at all. For the oceans have many secrets but tell none.

Paula's Pond was very fortunate it was sitting near the top of the newly created iceberg on which it now rode. The view was wonderful, except neither water nor ice can see very well, in fact, not at all. But being smaller had one distinct advantage. This smaller glacier could travel much faster than the larger ones from which it had peeled away. Off went the new iceberg, now free to ride where the ocean winds and currents chose to direct it. But a funny thing happens when an iceberg leaves the glacial nest, so to speak. It also leaves the great icebox that kept it cold. That's what started to happen to the iceberg. The block of ice seemed, at first, immune to change, but as the sun shone upon the ice mountain and the warm ocean water lapped against its white foothills and icy shoreline, the iceberg began shedding its ice in the form of cold water. The melting occurred slowly at first but seemed to speed up as the iceberg grew smaller.

Paula's Pond felt the change and must have begun to worry about becoming a part of the ocean and wanted very much not to be something so miniscule within something so vast. The pond was used to being made up of fresh water and had no use for sharks or octopuses, or even nasty squids having a tendency to ink things up in one way or another. Day by day the little pond felt her home growing smaller and the surface of the ocean getting closer as the iceberg sank into the sea. The pond didn't like what was happening one bit. Pieces of trees that had been a part of the iceberg floated away, and lots of the lovely boulders and rocks the pond collected in its travels were dropping from it and sinking into the depths of the ocean. This was not a good thing, for the pond considered all rocks and trees and bushes as part of its very being and was quite sad that all of the neat treasures it had tucked away over the many years were being slowly stolen away.

The iceberg floated around the ocean for months, all the while getting smaller and smaller. Paula's Pond accepted its doom now, aware that, like it or not, it soon would be swimming with the fishes, including sharks and octopuses and nasty squids. But incredibly, a large mass of land appeared over the horizon one morning just as Paula's Pond began to feel the salty waters of the ocean tickling its bottom. There arose a strong offshore current that carried the iceberg closer to the land, and as luck would have it, just about the time Paula's Pond snapped from the main iceberg, it was shoved like a helpless raft toward the large mass of land.

A loud roaring sound from somewhere beyond the shore grew louder and louder as the little iceberg raft drew nearer. The roar turned into a howling, and the wind picked up, blowing with all its might against the side of the little iceberg. The roar came from a tremendous river just now forming by the melting of many other glaciers hundreds of miles upstream. The water of the river moved with fury as it carved its way through the hills and valleys toward an unknown destination. As the little iceberg approached the shore, it was doomed to slam against the rocky shore and become stuck and then melt, quite a sad ending for one having traveled courageously for hundreds of miles. But fate intervened, and as the waters of the ocean slammed against the jagged shoreline, the little iceberg felt itself lifted high into the air and catapulted over a vast stretch of land, plummeting into the fury of the raging river. The river happily accepted the iceberg as if it were its child and allowed it to ride on its back for mile after mile as the raging waters hurled toward some unknown fate ahead.

After four days the iceberg was still floating on the river, somewhat smaller now but still massively content in knowing it wasn't floating around aimlessly in the ocean anymore. Then suddenly, a minor miracle occurred. At a sharp bend in the river, the water on the inside of the bend slowed to a crawl, but the outside of the bend shot forward with the force of a cannon. The little iceberg was hurled by the sudden force of this water high into the air and tumbled to the ground on the far side of the river. The iceberg bounced once, then twice, and then thrice before finding itself sitting comfortably in a piece of sunken ground which, by happenstance, would hold all the water it possessed! Content now it would not be a home to sharks or octopuses or even nasty squids, the ice happily nestled in its new home to melt. It would soon be home to wonderful things like fish and frogs and other creatures that were not now and never ever would be any kind of nasty. But what the little iceberg did not know was in its ice, it carried a mysterious cargo, not of rocks or trees or even bushes, but one something quite unexpected. The secret cargo would shake the very souls of a duo who discovered the secret centuries later—a friendly white squirrel named Lily and a little pink dragon named Mozart. And this is where the second half of our story begins.

A terrible storm descended upon the Great Green Forest one night. The wind had howled and surged across the sky like some insane monstrosity, and the clouds opened up, dropping rain by the bucketsful. All the animals of the forest had gone into hiding long before the storm struck, for their instincts told them a fierce and dangerous calamity was soon to be upon them. During the storm, dozens of trees fell to the ground, their hard fall unheard over the crash of lighting and the roar of thunder. Bushes torn from their roots rolled across the forest until they came to rest against a tree or another bush not uprooted by the fury of the storm. Thousands of leaves swirled in the sky like giant flocks of birds, and in the rush of the wind, large branches tore from high trees and fell where they would eventually rot and add to the richness of the soil on the floor of the forest. And over time other trees and bushes could grow and receive nourishment from them.

The storm passed now with the coming of the new day, and all the forest creatures ventured out, for their instincts told them it was safe to do so. On the bank of a small pond once part of a glacier stood a white squirrel and a little pink dragon.

"Wow!" Lily exclaimed, looking around at the forest. "That was some storm, Mozart, wasn't it?"

"It certainly was, Lily," the pink dragon replied, looking around at the debris on the ground. "It's just a good thing Mother Nature gave us great instincts to run to safety before the storm struck or we'd have been in real trouble."

As Mozart spoke, the two looked to the skies and watched as hundreds and hundreds of birds flew overhead. They formed a long line, and there were many different kinds of birds. Leading the vast armada of wings was Einstein the Wise Old Owl.

"They're back!" Lily squealed with delight. "The birds have returned!"

All the birds of the Great Green Forest sensed an impending doom was upon them and scattered to the four winds hours before the storm hit. Now they knew the storm had passed and it was safe to return to their homes. As they flew through the sky, they chirped and tweeted and cawed, letting all the forest creatures know they were safe and coming home.

"Listen to all those sounds!" Mozart replied. "It's like music to my ears."

Mozart's comment was true, for the forest had been hauntingly quiet on this morning after the storm. It was silent and still, for the bird songs usually heralding the dawn each morning and throughout the day had not been heard. But the sounds now returned in their fullness, and the reds and the blues and the greens and all the other majestic colors adorning the birds would enhance the colors of the trees. Mozart looked out over the now tranquil waters of Paula's Pond, the surface now littered with floating debris from the storm. Carl the Carp poked his head above the water and greeted them.

"Man, that was some storm!" Carl declared. "I usually don't feel these things under water, but the pond was rocking last night, I can tell you! I was bouncing up and down and all around by that storm. Now I know how a cowboy feels on a bucking bronco! Wow, what a ride I had!"

Carl was a real asset in keeping Paula's Pond clean for the carp would eat anything he happened to find in the mud. He was a bottom feeder and was forever scouring the depths of the pond for any morsel of food he could find. Once he accidentally swallowed a wristwatch and had most definitely been ticked off. And it had been a real wake-up call for the fish the first time the alarm went off. Eventually, however, he managed to expel this hindrance with a tremendous burp, thanks to a special herb given to him by Einstein the Wise Old Owl.

Down the shoreline, coming right at them, waddled a beaver carrying a stick in his mouth. When the animal got closer, he dropped the stick and spoke.

"Unbelievable!" the beaver shouted. "What a storm!" He pointed to a mound of sticks in the water. "That's what's left of my house! See, the roof has been ripped right off! It's going to take me days to get this darn thing fixed!"

The beaver had a most peculiar name. It was Pine-Oak-E-O, if you can believe it. Apparently, his mother had quite a sense of humor and thought it would be very funny to name her son after a wooden boy from a fable. Perhaps, one day realizing where his name came from, the animal began whittling. Now the beaver much preferred whittling with a small carving knife rather than risk damaging his enormous buckteeth gnawing on wood all day.

Lily noticed all the debris floating on the surface of the pond. "Hey, Pine-Oak-E-O," she offered. "Why go to the forest to get sticks? Look at all those branches floating on the water. They're all close to your house. Use them to fix your roof."

"Good idea, Lily," the beaver answered quickly, his big buckteeth gleaming in the morning sun. "That's the most excellent suggestion. There's enough wood out there to maybe even add on a room or two. I do need a game room when I have the boys over."

Lily, Mozart, and Pine-Oak-E-O stared at all the debris floating in the water.

"Hey!" Mozart shouted abruptly. "What's that?" The little pink dragon pointed one of his tiny claws in the direction of an object floating on the water. "It looks like a board—a great big board. What's that doing there?

"It does look like a board," Lily agreed. "Hey, Pine-Oak-E-O, how about swimming out and pushing it over here so we can take a look at it?"

"That's a big board," the beaver agreed. "I could use it in my house. Maybe it could be the very first board for my new game room."

The beaver ventured into the water and swam over to the board. He carefully turned the object around and swam in the direction of the shore. When he got there, he pushed the board on the bank so it wouldn't float away. As he emerged from the water, the beaver saw every animal staring down at the board.

"Why!" Mozart declared. "That's not a board at all! It's not even wood."

As if on command, the animals backed away from what the beaver had brought onshore.

"It's… it's… it's a Flat Person!" Lily shouted. "Run!"

All the animals turned and started to run away. A voice from above shouted, stopping them in their tracks.

"Stop running, you stupid ninnies!" the voice declared. "You don't have to run away!"

The voice came from Einstein the Wise Old Owl who was perched on the highest branch of a short tree not far from them. He looked down at the group.

"Why in the world are you running away?" he asked. "He's not going to bite you."

"He?" Pine-Oak-E-O asked.

"Yes, he," the owl explained. "Can't you see this is no board at all? It's a human wrapped up in a great big bandage. I'm sure he has no plans to burst out of it and eat any of you. He's not going anywhere, and he's probably been wrapped up in that outfit for centuries."

"Well, what's he doing here?" Mozart demanded. "In Paula's Pond, of all places. Where did he come from? Who is he? Why is he flat? And why is he all wrapped up?"

"I can't answer all those questions," the owl explained. "But I can answer some of them. It was a tremendous storm last night, the likes of which I have never seen before in the Great Green Forest." He pointed a wing toward the bandaged form on the ground. "I'm willing to bet our friend here has been resting at the bottom of the pond for quite a long time, buried in the mud. The storm churned up the mud last night and up he popped."

"That's amazing," Lily answered. "But what's he doing down there in the first place?"

Now what none of the animals knew, not even wise Einstein, was that the Flat Person hadn't always been flat. In fact, when his relatives had laid him to rest in all those bandages, he had been quite normal in shape. But he had been one of those things caught up in the ice when Paula's Pond was part of a moving mass of glacier. Over the centuries, the weight of the ice flattened the poor soul into what was as close to pancake flat as one could get. The bandages kept his body intact, and when the ice melted, he sunk to the bottom of Paula's Pond and was forgotten. The storm surge the previous night brought him to the surface.

"What are we going to do with Flat Person now?" Mozart asked.

"Well, I could use a surfboard," Pine-Oak-E-O joked. "My other one is made of wood."

"Funny," Einstein shot back sarcastically. "Really funny, Beaver. But there is only one decent thing we can do for this poor soul. That's to put him back where he came from."

"I don't want this creature in my pond!" Carl the Carp shouted. "Icky!"

"Oh, sure," Lily cut in. "Since when did you worry about swimming with anything icky. You spend all day sucking mud through your gills. And don't think we didn't see you munching on a dead skunk's leg a few months back. So don't 'icky' me."

Mozart addressed the owl. "What do we do now?"

"We'll put him back where he belongs. He's probably been down there for centuries. That's where his home is. We must give him a proper send off, one even his dear mother would be proud of. It is only right we do so, as good citizens of the forest."

And so it was done. One evening very soon afterward, when the surface of the pond was free of debris and the mud had settled back to the bottom, and the water was again a bright green, a ceremony was held. All the creatures of the Great Green Forest assembled on the shore and in the surrounding trees to watch the Flat Person return to the bottom mud of Paula's Pond from where he had risen. As the Flat Person rested on the shore, waiting to be moved, Einstein said a few words.

"Friends of the forest," he began in a booming voice. "We are all privileged to be here under a beautiful full moon this fine evening to wish our unknown friend, who we never had the privilege of meeting, good travel as he begins his journey once more. We know little about this man, but we can only assume he led a good life and was a gentle soul. That he chose to spend his afterlife in our pond is indeed a compliment to us all, and we should be proud he will forever reside near us. When we walk around the shoreline, or when we travel the sky above, or when we swim in these calm waters, we will forever pause to remember our departed friend and wish him Godspeed wherever his soul may be."

"I'm sure this Flat Person had a name at one time," Mozart said, his tone reflective, "just like all of us do. Perhaps we should give him a name now."

"Good idea," Einstein agreed. "How about Paul? That's an easy one to say."

"What if the Flat Person is a girl?" Lily asked. They all looked down at the Flat Person.

"We can't tell," Einstein pointed out. "Whatever he or she was has been flattened for a long time. Who's to say who the person was? Could have been a girl, there's no denying that." He put a wing under his chin, rubbing. "But I'm certainly okay with giving whoever it was a female name."

"How about instead of Paul, we call her Paula," Lily suggested.

"Okay," Einstein agreed. "But I wish we'd done this before my speech. My words addressed a guy, not a girl."

"Quite all right, Einstein," Pine-Oak-E-O said. "Your words were wonderful and inspiring, so it doesn't matter."

"Paula it is then," Lily said, grinning broadly. "Paula was my mother's name, if you remember, and it is in her memory we named this water Paula's Pond. It is a good name, and I'm sure my mother would gladly lend it to this poor soul. Thank you, Einstein."

"It is indeed fitting," the owl replied, "that the Flat Person's final resting place would be Paula's Pond since her name is now Paula. Funny how it all worked out." The owl turned to Mozart who stood in the midst of his Magical Mushroom Patch. "If you would do us the honor, friend Mozart."

With that the little pink dragon began to gently tap out notes with his little claws upon the tops of the mushroom caps. All around him and from the trees across the pond came the sweet sound of songbirds. The notes floated into the sky and skimmed the surface of the water. They rode the night breezes and slid down the faces of the forest animals, some of which stopped to scratch their noses or ears as the notes settled upon them and tickled their fancy.

As the ceremony continued and the sounds grew a little bit louder, Einstein motioned a wing to Pine-Oak-E-O the Beaver and Carl the Carp waiting next to the Flat Person. Einstein made a pushing motion toward the pond, signaling it was time to ease the Flat Person out onto the pond. Pine-Oak-E-O had been hesitant at first to push the Flat Person into the water. It meant having to put his nose right against the body until Einstein told him to think of the Flat Person as just another piece of wood. For in all probability, after spending all that time in the mud at the bottom of Paula's Pond, what the beaver was pushing probably more resembled something akin to wood than what it had been when it was living. Carl the Carp had no such hesitations, for he was quite used to shoving his nose into all sorts of stinky stuff at the bottom of the pond, and now secretly wanted to sneak a taste of the Flat Person should the opportunity avail itself.

The beaver and the carp headed out, gingerly pushing the Flat Person out into the open waters of Paula's Pond. Halfway across the pond floated a lily pad boat in which sat two other of the pond's inhabitants, the green bullfrogs Finnegan and Finagle. As the Flat Person came to a stop on the water, Pine-Oak-E-O lifted his tail from the water and placed it in the boat. The two frogs placed a large stone upon the beaver's tail and moved it until it rested over the Flat Person. The two frogs then leapt from their boat to the beaver's tail, carrying with them a strong rope. The beaver waited patiently as the two frogs wrapped the rope around the stone and secured it to the Flat Person. As the carp steadied the Flat Person, the frogs loosely knotted the rope and then signaled to the beaver to pull his tail out from between the stone and the Flat Person. When the beaver did so, the frogs deftly secured the rope so tightly even a sheet of paper could not fit between the stone and the Flat Person.

From the shore, satisfied the deed was done, Einstein motioned to Mozart, and as the little pink dragon began to play taps, the owl lowered his wing and the beaver and the carp let go of the Flat Person who sank, as one would expect, like a rock. As the Flat Person descended into the depths, a school of various fish waited. Immediately upon settling into the mud at the bottom of the pond, the fish furiously waved their tails all around the Flat Person, sweeping mud over the body until no sign of it could ever be detected.

But it is often said that during a moonlit night, the fog hovering over Paula's Pond at the exact spot where the Flat Person sank below the surface sometimes looks like a towering cloud over the water. Others claim, however, that if one squints their eyes really hard, the cloud seems more like a large block of ice.

CHAPTER 7

LILY AND ROBERT THE MOOSE

One bright sunny morning, Lily was playing in the Great Green Forest, jumping from tree to tree high above the forest floor, when she spotted something below her. As she drew closer to this curious sight, she found her good friend, Robert the Moose. Lily dropped to the forest floor and scurried over to the moose. And then she discovered something that astounded her—part of her friend seemed to be missing.

"Oh, no!" Lily moaned. "You poor dear, Robert! You've done it now! You've gone and lost your head! Are you out of your mind?"

"You silly squirrel," Robert replied. "My head is right here in this bush. Just follow my tail to my body, and take a sharp left when you come to my neck."

"I'll help you look for it," Lily said, quite relieved. "If your head is in the bush, it shouldn't be too hard to find it, especially if your antlers are still attached to it."

"I know very well where my head is, Lily," Robert assured the squirrel. "And I know where my antlers are too. My head is right on the end of my neck, where it's supposed to be, and my antlers sit just above them."

"Well," Lily replied, "if that truly is the case, Robert, then come on out of that bush and I can get a proper look at you. That is unless you've done something stupid to yourself."

"I would do what you ask, Lily, and gladly," Robert answered firmly. "But I am quite stuck inside this bush. My antlers are tangled hopelessly in these branches."

"Well, what is your head doing inside that bush?" Lily asked.

"If you must know," Robert answered, "I was after these yummy berries I found on this bush. I ate all the ones on the outside, so I was forced to poke my head further inside to find more of them. I guess I just got carried away when I found hundreds and hundreds of them deeper in the bush. To tell you the truth, they were quite excellent, even tastier than the berries on the outside branches."

Lily poked her head inside the bushes and, through the shadows, discovered, indeed, Robert's antlers were hopelessly tangled up, just as the moose had told her. Lily's sharp mind, thinking quickly, remembered she had just seen a picture show with her friend Mozart the Little Pink Dragon the evening before in the Open Glen Animal Theater. She thought about the movie now.

"Hey, I know!" Lily shouted joyfully, jumping around the bush. "I know how we can get you out of this mess!"

"You do?" Robert replied, quite surprised. "That's great! How?"

Over the years, Robert had grown skeptical of Lily's ideas for solving certain problems even though her intentions were always good, for the squirrel's solutions usually had more of a tendency not to solve a problem, but rather to complicate the matter.

"Yes, yes," the excited squirrel said, dancing on the branch. "I can help you, Robert! I truly can!"

Lily raised her two little white paws in front of her and squatted on her legs.

"I will free you with karate chops," she explained. Lily stood up on her legs and assumed the stance of a ninja warrior. "I just saw this in a movie."

"I don't think that's such a good idea," Robert answered as he observed his friend. "Lily, you don't know anything about karate, and you might hurt yourself. Worse yet, you might bonk me on the noggin with all the do-whack-a-do stuff you plan on doing."

"Not to worry, Robert," Lily shot back. "You just close your eyes and let me free you."

Robert did as Lily instructed and closed his eyes as a flurry of blows from Lily's paws slammed into the bush. More blows fell on the bush, and then more blows. Then it stopped, and Robert opened his eyes to find himself still entangled. Lily stood next to the bush, panting hard, her little paws full of pieces of bramble.

"This bush is tougher than I thought," she said. "Darn. Maybe I should be using my legs, for they are ten times more powerful than my paws."

"I don't think that's such a good idea," Robert replied, thinking a kick in the jaw from Lily's leg would hurt ten times more than a sock from her paw.

"Trust me, Robert, my friend," Lily said energetically. "This won't take long."

Now Lily's plan to use her feet to kick the branches away from the moose's antlers was a good one to her way of thinking. However, as Lily raised her foot to strike, she failed to realize that beneath the foot on which she now stood rested a very shiny and smooth large green branch quite slippery with berry juice dribbled from Robert's chin.

Just about the time Lily was about to strike the branch with her foot, she slipped on the wet branch and her foot missed her target entirely. But the squirrel knew she had kicked something, and hard. She quickly found out just what her foot had struck.

"Ouch!" said Robert the Moose. "And double ouch! That hurt!"

"Help," shouted Lily, her foot stuck firmly inside the bush. "Something's got me! Something's got my foot!"

"Lily, you nincompoop!" Robert groaned. "The bush hasn't got you. You have put your big foot in my ear!"

Lily peered into the bush and discovered Robert was right. Her foot was indeed stuck deeply inside of the moose's ear.

"Now get it out of there!" the moose demanded. "I told you this karate nonsense was a bad idea, and it was. See what you've done."

Lily leaned back and pulled on her foot. And she pulled a second time. Then she pulled once more, but to no avail. Her foot was stuck tightly deep inside Robert's ear.

"I hope you're happy with yourself now, Lily," Robert said, feeling the squirrel's foot squishing around inside of his ear. "This is just how I wanted to spend my day, tangled in a bush with a hairy white foot stuck in my ear. I'm just glad no one is around to see us like this."

As if on cue, they heard a piercing sound and looked up to see Elvis the Toucan Bird laughing at them, his black shock of hair quaking over his forehead as he laughed.

"Ha-ha-ha-ha!" Elvis howled. "I wish I had a camera right now, for this would make a really funny picture to show to all the forest animals. No one's going to believe this! You two will be the laughingstock of the forest!"

"Don't you dare tell anyone!" Robert warned. "I had nothing to do with this. This was all Lily's fault."

"Actually," Lily explained, "Robert got stuck in the bush all by himself. I was just trying to help get him out."

"Some help," Robert muttered to himself. "Good thing my tail's not stuck as well or this dumb squirrel would have cut it off by now."

"Perhaps I can help," Elvis offered.

The toucan fluttered from his high perch and into the bush. He landed next to them, his blue feet planted firmly on a branch. Elvis studied the plight of the moose and the squirrel and spoke.

"Why, with my scissors-like beak, I will cut you out of there in a jiffy," he assured them confidently. "And that will be that."

"You can?" Lily asked, her heart soaring at the bird's suggestion.

"I don't think that's such a good idea," Robert said.

"Oh, Robert," Lily scolded. "Don't be such a worry wart."

Elvis hopped from the branch and flew deeper into the bush.

"Are you ready?" Elvis asked, looking around. "Man, it is dark in here. You had both better close your eyes because there will be lots of bush stuff flying around when I begin cutting. I keep my beak sharp for moments just like this."

As Lily and Robert closed their eyes, they could hear Elvis slashing the bush with his beak. The sound was like music to their ears.

"Go, Elvis, go!" Lily encouraged. "Free us!"

After a few minutes, Elvis shouted in a surprised voice.

"Ouch, that was hard! That's real hard! What the heck is that?"

Robert and Lily opened their eyes to see what had happened to Elvis. Robert saw something hanging off the edge of Elvis' beak and shouted.

"You've bitten my antler, you stupid toucan!" he exclaimed. "You've cut some of my beautiful brown velvet off my tines."

"I don't think it's even noon yet," Elvis replied.

"I said 'tine,' not 'time', you idiot bird," Robert snorted. "A tine is a shaft of an antler that grows from the main stem, if you must know." Then he gave his head a tug and said, "And, with all your beak biting in here, I'm still tangled up in this dumb bush."

"Oh, Robert," Lily said, eyeing the antler. "It's just a little velvet Elvis bit off. I'm sure it will probably grow right back."

Robert looked over at Lily and began to laugh.

"What's so funny?" she demanded.

"Your birdbrained friend also visited you with his beak, Miss Grow Right Back," he grinned.

Lily felt her face and found the delicate white whiskers that grew so beautifully from the left side of her mouth had been cut off by a quick snip of the toucan's beak.

"My white whiskers!" she exclaimed. "My beautiful whiskers! They're gone!"

Lily was quite proud of her long white whiskers. When she shook her head, they shook as well and continued shaking long after her head stopped.

"Don't worry, Lily," Robert answered, mimicking what the squirrel had just told him. "It's just a few whiskers. They'll grow back. It doesn't matter that you will look funny for a while and will amuse a great number of the forest animals when they see you." Then he added with a chuckle. "Hey, Lily, I think your head is tilting a bit to the right even now. Maybe those missing whiskers made one side of your head lighter than the other."

51

Lily made a face at the moose.

"I'm just about finished," Elvis declared. "Just let me do a few more snips and you'll both be free."

"You are finished, you gooney bird!" Robert declared. "I'm not letting you cut any more of anything. Next time you'll probably hack my ear off or, worse yet, poke me in the eye."

In the sky above, Einstein the Wise Old Owl spotted the activity near the bush and flew down to investigate. He landed on top of the bush and settled his feathers, looking at the trio and pondering the situation. He looked into the bush.

"Why, Lily," he began. "What happened to your whiskers?"

Then the owl looked at Elvis.

"Elvis, why are you wearing Robert's velvet on your beak?"

Then he looked at Robert.

"Robert, why are you trying to hide your head in this bush? And what is Lily's foot doing in your ear?"

This seemed an awfully strange behavior to Einstein. Until this moment, the owl was sure he had witnessed all the weird things ever to happen in the Great Green Forest. But perhaps he was mistaken. This was something quite new. Lily, as one would expect, explained their plight to the friend who'd just joined them.

"Well, you see, Einstein," the squirrel muttered, trying to sound logical, "Robert got his antlers stuck in the bush while he was searching for berries, and I was going to hack him out with karate chops, but I slipped on a wet branch and got my foot wedged in his ear, and then Elvis was going to cut us out, but instead he clipped off some of Robert's antler velvet and then part of my beautiful whiskers. But after all of that, Robert is still stuck in the bush, and my foot is still stuck in Robert's ear. Robert won't let Elvis cut with his beak anymore because Robert is afraid he might lose an ear or maybe get a poke in the eye."

"Understandably so," the wise owl said calmly. "But perhaps I might be of some assistance to you in this matter."

Einstein fluttered down next to Robert's ear without a squirrel foot stuck in it and reached inside with his wing tip. He pulled out a gooey gob of yellow earwax and hopped over to Lily and dipped his wing into the other ear, smearing the wax onto Lily's ankle and foot.

"Now, rub hard, Lily," he ordered. "And let's see what happens."

Lily did as the owl commanded and felt her foot getting looser. She began moving her foot back and forth inside the moose's ear.

"Stop that!" Robert laughed, his body quaking. "That tickles!"

Lily felt her foot move within the moose's ear.

"It's almost free!" she shouted gleefully. "I can move it!"

"Almost is not quite good enough," Einstein answered. "And never will be."

With that the owl flew off, leaving the moose, the squirrel, and the toucan bird alone, wondering what he could do to help them. In a few moments, Einstein returned with Mozart the Little Pink Dragon on his back. Mozart brought with him a long, hollow reed with three holes cut in one side.

"You weren't kidding," Mozart chuckled, surveying the scene before him. "That squirrel is stuck."

"Okay, okay!" Robert said, not at all happy that more and more forest animals were getting involved in his predicament. "What is this dragon going to do to help us?"

"Mozart is going to set you free," Einstein explained. "He's going to finish the job."

"Oh, really," Elvis retorted. "You bring a dragon with a stick full of holes and expect something to happen. I still think I could just cut them out of there."

"No, no," Robert said, flicking his ear back, away from the toucan. "Let's hear what Einstein's plan is."

"Mozart is going to play his flute," Einstein said.

"Play his flute?" Robert asked, amazed by what Einstein had said. "You call that a plan? I thought you were a wise owl."

"I am a wise owl," Einstein answered confidently. "Wiser than most, I might add. Mozart is going to play his flute in your ear."

"In my ear!" Robert shouted. "In my ear! Don't you know Lily's foot is stuck in my ear?"

"I am well aware of that fact," Einstein calmly replied. "He will play the flute in your other ear, you silly moose. We will create a stiff wind and will help blow Lily's foot free from your other ear."

"That is a very stupid plan," Robert argued. "I'm not going to let anyone stick a flute in my ear."

"Pretty funny words coming from someone who let a squirrel stick her leg in one of their ears," Einstein said, motioning to Mozart. "Suit yourself, then. We'll just go home."

"Don't leave us here like this!" Lily pleaded to the moose. "Come on, Robert! What have you got to lose? I'm just about free."

"Let's see," Robert answered quickly. "What have I got to lose? I'm standing here with my antlers stuck in a bush. Some of my beautiful antler velvet is dangling from the beak of a toucan bird. To add to that, I've got the smelly foot of a squirrel shoved in my ear. You ask me what I've got to lose, Lily? Hel-l-l-l-o-o!"

"It's either Einstein's plan or we stay here all night," Lily explained. "And I'm supposed to go to the Open Glen Animal Theater tonight."

"Really?' Robert asked, momentarily forgetting his dilemma. "What's playing?"

"*Bambi*," Lily replied. "It's a good one."

"Oh, wow!" Robert shouted. "*Bambi*! What an awesome movie!"

"Can we stay focused here?" Einstein interrupted in a miffed tone. "You're not going anywhere unless you're both free."

Robert mulled over Einstein's words and realized he didn't want to spend the night like this. He did want to see *Bambi* now that he was aware the movie was playing.

"I guess a little music in my ear won't do much harm," the moose admitted reluctantly. "It might be soothing after everything that has happened to me today."

Einstein watched as Mozart poked the end of the flute into Robert's ear. Mozart puckered his lips and put his little dragon fingers over two of the flute's three holes. Mozart then took a deep breath and prepared to blow.

"This may be a little loud," Einstein warned.

Mozart blew into the flute with all the strength he could muster, his little dragon cheeks puffing out with all the wind his lungs could hold. The sound of the flute blasted through the air and roared into Robert's ear. Lily was in awe of the sound, for never in a million years could she imagine a little flute could make so much noise. Robert, his ear ringing from the noise, reared back and tore his body from the bush. He lifted his head high, shaking it back and forth, trying desperately to drive out the blaring blast echoing through his brain. The moose's violent shaking launched Lily into the sky like a cannonball, freeing her foot from the moose's ear.

"Holy unicorn horn!" Robert shouted, shaking his head so hard his antlers rattled. "That's loud! My ears hurt!"

"Robert, Robert!" Einstein yelled excitedly. "You're free! You're free!"

Robert stopped shaking and looked around, the ringing in his ears slowly fading away.

"I'm free!" he snorted with glee. "I'm free! I'm free of the bush and I'm free of Lily! Hoorah! Hoorah for me!"

It was quite a sight to behold. Robert stood next to the bush, scattered pieces of branches hanging from his antlers like green tinsel from a Christmas tree, his chin stained purple with berry juice. Elvis sat perched in a branch with some of Robert's antler velvet still dangling limply over the side of his beak. Mozart sat on the ground, holding a flute whose end was covered with a large gooey gob of Robert's earwax. Lily lay on the ground, shaken by her cannon blast from Robert's ear and dazed by her abrupt jolt as she landed hard on the forest floor. The foot formerly stuck in Robert's ear jutted into the air, covered with much more gooey gob than was stuck on the end of Mozart's flute.

Einstein looked around, satisfied with what he saw. He gave an approving hoot and spoke.

"You see," the owl explained, "every problem can be solved if you just use your head, and a dab of earwax."

"And a flute," Lily added as she stood up.

"And a flute," the owl repeated.

Mozart turned to Robert and spoke.

"Robert, why in the world did you stick your head into that bush, anyway?"

Now Mozart already knew why the moose was deep in the bush for Robert's chin, lips, tongue, and even the tip of his flat nose were all purple with berry juice. It was well known the moose possessed a short memory, and Mozart was just trying to have some fun at his friend's expense. Robert thought for a moment about what Mozart had asked.

"I don't know why," he said. "I knew a minute ago, but to tell you the truth, in all this excitement, I have forgotten why I stuck my head into that bush."

Robert walked over to the bush.

"But I will find out for you right now, Mozart. That I will do, my flute tooting friend."

Robert stuck his head deep into the bush and stared into the darkness.

"Did you find out why you stuck your head in that bush?" Elvis asked.

"Yes, I think I just did," Robert the Moose answered. "I believe it was to remind myself never to stick my head too far into a bush filled with thick branches and darkness."

"Very good," Einstein replied. "You learned something today. Now we all can go home."

"Not quite yet," Robert answered, embarrassed. "I'm stuck."

CHAPTER 8

LILY AND THE MISSING MUSHROOM PATCH

Early one morning Lily sat on the bank of the Rogue River, listening to the gentle rushing of the water flowing around the rocks in the riverbed. She was quite content as she munched on her favorite candy, a chocolate peanut cluster. As she munched, she considered sticking her feet into the cool running waters of the river but decided to wait. The water would be warmer in the afternoon, and she might find it more comfortable to do then. Suddenly, the silence of the morning was broken by a frantic voice.

"Help! Help!" the voice shouted. "Oh, help me! I've been robbed! Robbed I tell you! Robbed!"

Now Lily was leaning against a tree, listening to the water, but sat straight up and whirled around, anxious to see from where the voice was coming. To her amazement, she saw her friend, Mozart the Little Pink Dragon, running down the trail toward her as fast as he could. A cloud of dust kicked up behind the dragon as his tail dragged along the dirt.

"Help!" Mozart shouted at Lily. "Help me! I've been robbed, I tell you! Just plain robbed!"

"What is it?" Lily asked the little dragon. "Who robbed you?"

"I don't know! I don't know!" answered the befuddled Mozart. "But it's just terrible!"

Mozart grabbed Lily's paw and began to pull her down the trail from where he had come.

"Come and see! Come and see!" he said. "See what they have done, those rotten scoundrels! Just see what they've done to me!"

Mozart led Lily to a small clearing surrounded by bushes. In the small enclosure, Lily saw the Magical Mushroom Patch.

"I was afraid someone had stolen your Magical Mushroom Patch, Mozart," she said. "But see, it's right here where you left it."

"No!" Mozart explained, his voice wailing. "Look again! It's terrible!"

Mozart pointed to something in the middle of the mushroom patch. Lily saw what the dragon was pointing at.

"Oh, no" Lily gasped. She looked at Mozart. "I can't believe it!"

For you see, someone apparently had snuck in under the cover of the night and unscrewed the very soft cushioning caps of the two largest mushrooms. What remained were the two stout pedestals that used to hold the caps. The stems looked quite lonely now and were certainly in no condition to play music.

"Who would do something like this?" Mozart moaned. "Who would dare?"

What made the Magical Mushroom Patch magical in the first place was the music played by banging on the caps of the mushroom, and Mozart played music to delight the forest animals almost every day. But now, with two of the mushroom caps missing, the little pink dragon could play no music, at least no decent melodies, and therefore the Magical Mushroom Patch was no longer magical.

"We will find whoever did this," Lily assured the dragon. "I promise. We will get those rogues, and we will get your mushroom caps back where they belong."

Off Lily and Mozart trotted, searching the forest for the culprits who had stolen the caps off the tops of the magical mushrooms. They asked Freddie the Indian, Einstein the Wise Old Owl, and even Elvis the Toucan Bird, but none of them had seen anyone carrying the mushroom caps, and none of the three had the vaguest idea what one would do with a mushroom cap that size anyway. In the early afternoon, Lily and Mozart grew tired from their search.

"Let's go down and sit by Paula's Pond," Lily suggested, knowing the gentle lapping of the water against the shore would calm them. "We can relax for a while and then search for the mushroom caps after we rest a bit. It will do us both some good."

"Fine," answered Mozart. "But let's not rest too long. Who knows what the culprits plan to do with my mushroom caps. They might use them as a hat or even a bowl for cereal. Or, worse yet, they might cut them up for food. How sad that would be."

Mozart was anxious to find the missing mushroom caps, for he knew there would be no music in the Great Green Forest until the Magical Mushroom Patch was complete once more. The pair began to walk toward the pond.

"Look!" Mozart suddenly shouted, pointing to the ground. "Would you just look at that!"

Lily saw he pointed to something like fine fairy dust sparkling on the ground, and she remembered the tops of each mushroom cap also had sparkling dust on them. The pair began to follow the trail of sparkle. As they rounded a bend in the trail leading to the pond, Mozart pointed his finger at something.

"Look!" he shouted angrily. "There are the missing mushroom caps! And there sit the two scoundrels who stole them!"

Lily looked to where the dragon pointed by the edge of the pond where the trail of sparkle ended abruptly. Just as the dragon had declared, sitting at the water's edge were the two missing mushroom caps. And sunning themselves on top of the mushroom caps, as if floating on soft pillows, were her two green frog friends, Finnegan and Finagle, their little rear ends sparkling with dust where they sat on the mushroom caps.

"Hey, get off of those!" Mozart shouted to the frogs.

The two frogs turned and stared at the little dragon for a minute and then without a word closed their eyes and continued to sun themselves on the mushroom caps. Lily and Mozart walked over to the frogs and stood between them and the sun.

"Hey, you're blocking my sunlight," Finnegan said, opening his eyes to look at them. "Can't you see I'm working on my tan? You're in the way of my rays."

Mozart grew very irritated.

"Your tan!" he shot back, drawing his little dragon claw into a fist. "A frog with a tan! I'll give you a tan all right! I'm about to give you a tanning like you've never had before, you little mushroom cap thief! And that tan's not going to go on your face!"

"Thief?" Finnegan asked, with an air of boredom in his voice. "Why, whatever do you mean calling little old me a thief?"

"You heard me!" Mozart continued. "Not only are you a thief, but your little green friend next to you was probably in on it, too."

"In on what?" Finagle asked, somewhat irritated by this whole conversation. "Whatever are you talking about?"

Mozart pointed to the mushroom caps on which the frogs sat.

"Those," he said. "You took those mushroom caps from my Magical Mushroom Patch."

"What if we did?" Finnegan said. "After all, they were just lying around on the ground."

"They were most assuredly not lying on the ground," Mozart insisted. "When I left the Magical Mushroom Patch last night, the mushroom caps were screwed tightly on their pedestals just like they are supposed to be."

"Are you sure you frogs found the mushroom caps on the ground?" Lily asked.

Finnegan shot a look at Finagle.

"Well, maybe not so much," he said. "But they were close to the ground when we found them. Maybe we kind of helped them go the rest of the way."

"Helped them!" Mozart shouted. "What did you two nasty frogs do?"

"We're not nasty frogs," Finagle answered. "We were just hopping through the forest, heading to Paula's Pond for our early morning swim, when we found the mushroom patch just sitting by itself, sparkling nicely in the morning sun. Then we hopped on top of the two biggest mushrooms and just sort of got the hankering to dance. We found if we danced really hard, the mushroom caps would spin and all sorts of twinkles would bounce up and then fall back onto the cap. It was quite an exhilarating experience."

"And you danced so hard you unscrewed the mushroom caps?" Lily asked. "Is that your story?"

"That's right," Finnegan agreed. "You may be unaware frogs dance counterclockwise in a circle, and that motion must have been what loosened the mushroom caps from their stems. When we realized the caps were about to fall, we hopped off to save ourselves just as they fell to the ground. We got off just in the nick of time." Then he added sarcastically, "By the way, thanks for your concern about our safety. Very touching."

"And when we saw them laying there," Finagle continued, "we thought they would make excellent sunning seats next to the pond. I mean, why let these beautiful sparkling caps just sit on the ground and rot like leaves? You know we frogs must sun ourselves every day to keep our skins the pretty green you see here." The frog glanced down to admire his skin. "We set the caps on their edges and wheeled them over here so we wouldn't have to sit in the dirt when we sunned ourselves. And until you two got here and blocked the sunshine, everything was going just peachy." The frog turned to Mozart. "You see, my little pink friend, we didn't steal anything."

"That's ridiculous," Mozart snorted, puffs of pink smoke erupting from his nostrils. "I must have those mushroom caps back!"

"Sorry," Finnegan answered calmly. "You see, we rather like these mushroom caps. The sun warms them quite nicely, and they are so soft to sit on. You know what they say—finders keepers. And, as an added bonus, they make music, too."

With that said, Finnegan raised his leg and kicked at the mushroom cap on which he sat. A very dull note came from somewhere deep inside of the mushroom.

"See what I mean," he said.

Finagle then raised his leg and kicked at his mushroom. It played a note as well, but much different than how Finnegan's note sounded.

"See," he said. "Pretty cool, huh?"

"But I'm afraid you'll have to give the mushroom caps back," Lily explained to the frogs, "for Mozart cannot play music and sing for the animals of the forest unless the Magical Mushroom Patch is back as it was before. The rest of the forest animals will be quite disappointed if that happens, and Mozart will be extremely sad he cannot play concerts for them. Can't you see that?"

Finnegan and Finagle thought about what Lily said.

"Okay, Lily," Finnegan offered, "we will give them back on one condition, and that is, if you can find something suitable to replace them with, something as comfortable where we can sun ourselves, preferably something that plays music as well, so we can catch our groove as we take in some rays."

"Why, I'll groove you!" Mozart shouted. "You silly pieces of fish bait! And I'd like to tell you where you can stick your rays! Why, I ought to tell Eddie the Eagle where you are! You'd soon find yourselves warming yourselves in his stomach! That would fix the both of you."

"Sticks and stones," the frogs said in unison, and then Finagle added, "but you're not getting these mushroom caps until you bring us something to replace them with. And that's that."

Realizing the frogs weren't going to budge from the mushroom caps, Lily made a decision.

"Let's get out of here, Mozart," the squirrel said. "Surely there must be something in the forest that we could find for these two yahoos to plop their lazy green rear ends on other than your mushroom caps."

Lily and Mozart looked around the forest for a while but were disappointed when they could find nothing suitable to trade with the frogs for the mushroom caps. The frogs wouldn't like wood or branches or anything like that as much as they liked the mushroom caps. Finally, Lily had an idea.

"I know," she said. "Let's go over and talk to Freddie the Indian. He's always making something clever, and perhaps he will do the same for us."

Lily and Mozart soon arrived at the Indian's home and found Freddie inside of his teepee singing opera in a very loud and deep voice.

"What are you doing in there, singing like that, Freddie?" Lily asked.

"Oh, hi, Lily," Freddie answered from inside. "I'm taking a bubble bath, and I always sing opera when I bathe. Oh, the water is nice and warm, too. The bubbles kind of bring out the artistic flair in me. But I don't have my loincloth on right now, so don't you dare come in here."

Lily and Mozart looked around at the area outside of Freddie's tepee. All sorts of Freddie's clever inventions lay scattered on the ground. They found Freddie's walnut bat, a very long stick with big leaves on the end so Freddie could bat walnuts down from high in the trees. They played with a fish fooler, a piece of clay Freddie had fashioned into a fat worm so the fish would bite on it. They tested out Freddie's skyscraper, a long pole with thin sticks on the end Freddie used to fool the young forest animals with, telling them he could scrape the spider webs from the sky to keep it blue. There were lots of things like this, and as the squirrel and the dragon looked around, Lily's foot rubbed against two round metal rings stacked one on top of the other. Between the rings ran a thin band of wood fashioned in a circle, and several smaller metal disks were secured to narrow slits in the wood. The metal and wood were held together with a thick piece leather string. The clever Indian had constructed two of these. A musical note escaped from one of the objects when Lily's foot moved it.

"Hey, Freddie," Lily shouted, holding up one of the objects. "What's this?"

Freddie stuck his bubble-encrusted head through the flap of the tepee and looked at what Lily held in her hand.

"Oh, that," he replied. "I made those just recently. I call it a *timborine*."

"A timborine?" Lily asked.

"Yes," Freddie answered. "Because I made it from timber. Those little metal disks fastened in the wood slits I call clackers because I happened to be eating crackers when the idea came to me."

Calling something a clacker just because one happened to be eating crackers made no sense to Lily, but she went with the flow.

"Well, what do you do with it?" Lily asked.

"Pick it up and bang it against your paw," Freddie instructed and then pulled his head back inside to continue his bath.

Lily did as the Indian told her to do and was amazed at the many musical sounds she heard as she banged her paw at various places around the metal bands. The metal disks jingled in the wood and made the sounds. Mozart picked up the second timborine and banged it against his hip.

"Hey," the dragon smiled, moving his hips back and forth. "This is very clever. As a lover of all things musical, I'd say this is pretty darn cool."

Mozart and Lily began banging harder on the timborines. They were soon dancing to the music they were making as they banged the timborines over their heads. Suddenly Lily stopped.

"Hey," she said. "I've got a great idea. Why don't we trade these to the frogs for your mushroom caps?"

"That's a great idea," Mozart agreed. "But didn't they want something they could sit on as well as play music with?"

"You are right, Mozart," Lily replied. "They did say as much."

She looked around the area and spied an object hanging on Freddie's clothesline.

"Oh, boy," she said. "Have I got a great idea."

Lily shouted to her big Indian friend still bathing in the warmth of his teepee.

"Hey, Freddie, do you suppose I can have these timborines?"

"Sure, Lily," Freddie answered proudly. "Take them both. I can always make more. I'm glad you like them."

Lily had also spotted Freddie's loincloth drying on the clothesline. Lily knew the loincloth was made of soft leather. She knew that with Freddie's loincloth, she could make the one thing she needed to get the mushroom caps away from the frogs.

"Okay," she explained to Mozart, "here's what we're going to do. We will make some sunning seats for the frogs from these timborines. We will cover the tops of them with leather and secure them with a vine. Then we will trade the frogs these musical timborines for the mushroom caps."

"Are you sure this is going to work?" Mozart asked. "Where are we going to get soft leather to cover these?"

"Let me worry about that," Lily said.

Then Lily turned toward the tepee.

"We're leaving, Freddie," she said. "By the way, you certainly have some fine things here."

"Oh, thank you," Freddie answered as he poured more bubble bath on himself inside of the tent, singing a few opera notes as he did so. "Feel free to borrow anything you like."

That being said, Lily immediately ran to the clothesline and pulled Freddie's loincloth from the rope on which it hung. Mozart's mouth dropped open.

"Lily!" he cried. "You're going to take Freddie's loincloth? Is nothing sacred?"

Mozart knew Freddie wore only a loincloth to cover himself, and he was shocked Lily would have the audacity to take it right off the clothesline.

"He did say to borrow anything we'd like, didn't he?" Lily defended. "He said it clear as day. I'll find him another one somehow." She stared into the dragon's eyes. "You *do* want to get your mushroom caps back, don't you, Mozart?"

As the squirrel and the dragon scurried off with their newfound loot, Freddie peeked through the flap in his tent and gasped. A very angry voice boomed through the woods.

"Somebody has stolen my clothes!" Freddie shouted. "Help! There's a loincloth thief loose in the forest!"

"Think this will work?" Lily asked Mozart later as she held up a thick piece of vine she had retrieved from the woods.

"Yes, that's perfect, Lily," Mozart replied.

Mozart was quickly changing his mind about the Indian's loincloth. *Perhaps this plan of Lily's would work.* The dragon was a little leery about Lily cutting the leather into two pieces, but he managed to get over it in short order. Lily wound the vine around the sides of the timborine as Mozart stretched the leather over the hole on the top. The timborine now looked a bit like a drum, except for the little metal disks on the side, which made music when the instrument was shaken or slapped.

"Oh, this will do quite nicely," Lily nodded approvingly as she admired their work. "Quite nicely, indeed."

67

They repeated their work on the second timborine. After they checked to make sure the vines were tight, they dipped the timborines into the waters of Paula's Pond and then set the two instruments in the sun to dry. When the sun warmed the leather, the material shrank and tightened like the face of a drum. After waiting two hours, Lily and Mozart were satisfied with the results of their work and picked up the timborines. Then they set off to find the frogs on the other side of the pond.

"What have you got there?" Finnegan asked when he saw the squirrel and dragon approaching with the instruments. The frog was suspicious for he had never seen such objects before. "What are those funny looking things?"

"Your new sunning seats," Lily explained. "They are much nicer than those mushroom caps."

"Oh, yea," Finagle smirked, as only a frog can. "Let's see you prove it. I have grown quite fond of my sunning seat, and I'm not sure I want to give it up."

"These are way better," Lily explained, winking at Mozart. "And we will prove it."

As the two frogs watched, Lily and Mozart set the timborines on the ground and stood on them.

"You see," she said. "You can sit on these and sun yourselves."

"So what," Finnegan said. "We can do the same with these."

Mozart kicked his timborine, and music came from the metal attached to the wood.

"See," he said, "these make music, too."

"Big deal," Finagle scoffed. "So do these."

With that, Finagle kicked at her mushroom cap and made a note come out.

"Well," Lily said, "I guess we'll just have to keep these timborines. But that's okay because I sure would miss playing on them." Then she added. "Anyway, keep those mushroom caps. They're last year's model and probably out of date anyway. Mozart was just about to order some new ones. So you frogs can just keep them until they fall apart."

She began to bounce up and down on the new leather that had, until quite recently, been Freddie the Indian's loincloth. The frogs, seeing the white squirrel bouncing high into the sky, took notice. With each bounce, fun noises came from the timborines.

"Hey," Finnegan said in an amazed voice, "that looks like fun. Let us try."

"Sorry," Lily answered. "You can only jump on them if you own them."

By now, both frogs were drooling, for jumping was their favorite thing to do. It's what the frogs lived for. And right before them were two instruments tailor-made just for frogs.

"Lily said these are last year's models," Finnegan whispered to Finagle while eyeing the mushroom caps. "Do we really want something so old that's going to wear out quickly? Then we'd have nothing at all."

"That would be most mortifying," Finagle answered as he watched Lily bounce and heard notes coming from the timborine. "Not quite the level of sophistication one would expect out of a frog."

"I quite agree," Finnegan said. "Imagine if we were dancing on those nasty old mushroom caps and leapt into the air and when we landed, our feet went through the darn things."

"How embarrassing!" both frogs cried in unison.

The pair turned to Lily and Mozart. "Okay, okay," Finagle said anxiously. "Give us the timborines, and we'll give you back the mushroom caps. Fair enough?"

"Fair enough," Mozart said reluctantly. He winked at Lily. "But you're getting the better deal here, you sly frogs."

Thus, the trade was made on the shore of Paula's Pond. As Lily and Mozart rolled the mushroom caps back to the Magical Mushroom Patch, they looked back to see the two happy frogs gleefully bouncing up and down on the soft leather. And as the frogs landed on the leather, joyous musical sounds arose with each froggy bounce.

When Lily and Mozart arrived back at the Magical Mushroom Patch, they quickly lifted the mushroom caps back on their pedestals and screwed them down tightly. Mozart grabbed a pair of drumsticks and immediately began banging on one of the caps, making sure no damage resulted from the reckless dancing of the frogs' feet. He smiled at Lily, and it was then Lily knew the mushrooms were as good as new. But her smile was interrupted by an angry voice.

"Hey, loincloth thieves!"

Lily and Mozart were startled to see Freddie the Indian looming over them, holding a dripping bath towel around his waist. Bubbles surrounded his long black hair and stuck to his cheeks. The Indian smelled as sweet as the flowery aroma of the bath he had hurriedly deserted. Freddie did not look at all happy.

"What did you two do with my loincloth you stole from my clothesline?" he demanded. "My beautiful, soft leather loincloth."

"Well, well," Lily said, directing her comment toward Mozart, fully aware the Indian was watching them. She pointed at Freddie. "There stands the Most Magnificent Hero of the Great Green Forest."

The Indian was at first flattered by Lily's unexpected compliment but then thought better of it.

"Now don't try any double talk on me, Lily!" Freddie warned. "I had to sneak halfway through the forest looking for you two scoundrels. And dressed like this to boot."

"Well, I don't think anyone would mind how you look," Lily assured him, "especially after what you did for all the animals of the forest who live here."

"What did I do?" Freddie asked, puzzled. "Whatever did I do?"

"Oh, Freddie," Lily replied happily. "You always were the humble one, weren't you? Why, without you giving up your loincloth, we could never have gotten the missing mushroom caps back. Without them, the Magical Mushroom Patch would have been gone forever. The music from the mushrooms would have never been heard in the forest again. It would be like you not being able to sing opera during your bubble bath. You are a true forest hero."

Freddie gasped as he thought about what the squirrel said. As Lily spoke, she saw lots of animals were now gathering nearby to hear her words.

"Let's hear it for Freddie the Indian, the Most Magnificent Hero of the Great Green Forest!" she shouted. "Hip, hip, hoorah! Hip, hip, hoorah!"

As the cheers rose from the animals, Freddie forgot all about the fact Lily had taken his loincloth from the clothesline and left him with nothing to wear. As they all sat down around the mushroom patch, Mozart began to bang on the mushroom caps and right on the spot made up a ballad about the generosity of their wonderful Indian friend, Freddie:

Oh, let me tell you about Freddie, our dear Indian friend
Who gave up his loincloth that covered his end
He is so giving
And also forgiving
He's like a big teddy
We love our dear Freddie

All of the forest animals joined in and sang too, not comprehending why all of a sudden their Indian friend had become the Most Magnificent Hero of the Great Green Forest but not wanting to miss out on the opportunity to be part of a sing-along either. So they just sang:

Oh, let us sing about Freddie, our dear Indian friend
We needed a favor and from that he did not bend
Our little timborine, we really had to mend
And it was so nice of Freddie to us lend
That little piece of leather swinging in the breeze
But will no more rub against his little Indian knees

All the animals laughed as Freddie's face turned bright red. Late into the night they sang and played some more. And it didn't matter much to Freddie that all he wore around his waist was a wet bath towel. The bath bubbles on his face had long since burst, and he knew he wore the fragrance of flowers from his bath. He was among his friends and felt content.

Tomorrow he would make another loincloth.

CHAPTER 9

LILY RESCUES MICHAEL THE ANGEL

One evening, just before sunset, Lily decided to take a walk in the Great Green Forest along one of the many paths leading to Paula's Pond. It was a very warm evening, and Lily was feeling very good about all the smiles she had given away that day. The great thing about smiles, Lily knew, was that you could give them away freely, and, unlike broken merchandise, smiles are never taken back. Lily walked for a while and rounded a bend in the path, and there, on the floor of a little valley below her, sat the pond. Lily saw the calm water, the surface of the pond catching the last rays of the setting sun. The rays bounced happily from the glassy surface and rose to greet her.

Lily decided to walk down to the edge of the pond and sit on the large round boulder next to the shore. There were many rocks of all sizes around Paula's Pond, and some of them took the shape of animals and the like, but most of them were round. This particular rock was her favorite place to sit because it was the largest, and when she climbed up it, she was treated to a grand view. The rock was smooth and usually quite warm and cozy near sunset from absorbing the sun's heat all day. But as Lily approached the rock, she was shocked by something already on top of it, a stranger never before seen in the Great Green Forest.

Lily looked up, awed by the figure before her. On top of the rock stood a tall, almost ghostly white figure, the whitest white Lily had ever seen, and that was saying something, for Lily sported her own immaculately white fur coat, the whitest thing in the Great Green Forest. And this great figure had wings! Lily realized now it was an angel, something she'd only heard about before now and a rather tall one because it stood at least seven feet tall! And seven feet of anything, particularly standing on a huge boulder, is very tall to a little squirrel that, even on a windless day, could barely scrape up eight inches of height. Lily pondered running away but summoned the courage to move forward. She eased over to the boulder, casting a glance at the figure's reflection off the surface of Paula's Pond as she moved.

"Who are you?" Lily asked in the bravest voice she could muster.

"Why, Lily," the figure replied, rather surprised at her question. "You already know me, don't you? I'm Michael and I'm an angel." The figure pointed to his back. "That would explain these wings, wouldn't it, little squirrel?"

"Really?" Lily inquired, not knowing what to make of everything she was seeing. "How do you know my name?"

"Your name is written on the surface of your soul, and I can see it right there," the angel said, pointing toward the squirrel's heart. "And to answer your first question, again, I am Michael and I am most definitely an angel."

"Well," Lily continued, "if you are this Michael the Angel, what are you doing on this rock? I mean, this is Earth and it's almost sunset. Aren't you supposed to be in heaven guarding something?"

"My, you are certainly an inquisitive little thing, aren't you?" Michael the Angel said with a smile. "I like that. But I do suppose I present quite a sight, standing here on this rock."

"Well, you do kind of look like a statue," Lily said. "You are on a pedestal and look like you're made of white marble, very pretty white marble though." Then she added, "What are you doing on this rock, anyway?"

"Well," Michael answered. "Why don't you just jump up here with me and I'll tell you. There's plenty of room up here for the both of us."

Lily scampered up the boulder and stood close to the angel who looked down at her.

"Well," Michael began, "just let me tell you then. I was flying over the Great Green Forest on my way to the urgent business of telling a very worried mother her extremely sick child was going to get well soon, regardless of how things looked right now. I was running a bit late, and I should have been paying closer attention—you know how the weather over a body of water can change quickly. Sure enough, a big gust of wind blew up from this pond and tore off my Gold Feather, and I was forced to land as best I could. I ended up stranded on this rock."

"Your Gold Feather?" Lily asked.

"Yes," Michael the Angel replied, pointing to a spot high on his left wing near his shoulder. "See here. There's a feather missing."

Sure enough, a feather was missing from the top of the angel's left wing. Lily could see clearly a narrow hole where a feather was supposed to be.

"But what's so special about this feather?" Lily asked. "After all, you've got hundreds of feathers on your wings. And they are all so beautiful." Lily touched the angel. "And they go well with this robe you're wearing." The robe felt like silk to the squirrel, soft and white with a sweet fragrance not of this earth.

Lily looked at the angel's wings. The feathers were all arranged neatly in rows with the tip of each feather pointing toward the ground. The feathers were mostly white with just a tinge of light blue showing where the end of each feather was connected to the wing. Each feather glimmered in the fading sun, but between feathers, Lily saw warm glowing lights, barely discernable, and the glows slowly changed colors from soft blues to pinks and then back again. Lily thought of her pink dragon friend Mozart and how he would enjoy watching the pink glow coming from the angel's wings. Only the spot where the Gold Feather was missing remained dark, the hole seeming to grow larger as darkness fell.

"But none of these feathers are gold," Michael answered, glancing at his wings. "The gold one is the one that holds my power so I am able to fly."

"Well, where did the feather go?" Lily asked.

"I'm afraid it fell into this pond," Michael said, bowing his head sadly. "I need to find it before dawn. If I don't find it, then everyone will see me standing out here on this rock. It just wouldn't look very good for us angels if one of us couldn't fly. It would kind of ruin our image, if you know what I mean. When an angel doesn't do what he's supposed to, it makes the news worldwide. Good news never hits the paper, but bad news always does, you know."

"I see," Lily replied. "Perhaps we could help you look for your lost Gold Feather."

Lily noticed the glowing lights on the angel's wings fading a bit and thought that was probably a good thing. Glowing lights in the darkness would attract a crowd, and that wasn't what was needed now. What was needed was the lost Gold Feather.

"Would you, Lily?" Michael asked. "You would be such a dear and help a poor angel?"

"Certainly," Lily answered. "You angels are always helping us out one way or the other, whether we know it or not. Now could be our chance to repay some of those good deeds with a good deed of our own."

Michael looked toward the heavens.

"I know many would be most grateful to you, Lily."

"You just wait right here until I get back," Lily instructed, looking around. "I am going to get some help."

Without waiting for Michael to answer, Lily turned and scurried off into the forest, not stopping until she stood at the base of the tree where Einstein the Wise Old Owl lived. Lily looked up to see Einstein stirring in his sleep. Sometimes the owl went to bed early, and this, apparently, was one such night. But Lily would have none of it.

"Wake up, Einstein!" Lily shouted. "Wake up, good friend!"

Mozart the Little Pink Dragon also heard Lily's shout and flittered over clumsily to see what all the commotion was about. The little dragon's wings weren't built for flying, but occasionally Mozart managed to lift off the ground.

"What's up, Lily?" Mozart asked. "What's all the fuss?"

"Yea, what's all the fuss?" Einstein snorted from his perch above them.

"Please come with me!" Lily pleaded. "I need your help."

"What is the problem, Lily?" Einstein asked, yawning. "I'm in for the night."

"You've got to come with me!" Lily explained. "There's an angel down by Paula's Pond, and he needs help."

Einstein and Mozart looked at each other for a moment and then burst into laughter.

"Oh, Lily," Mozart snickered, "an angel by the pond. That's a good one."

"Just one angel?" Einstein teased. "You saw only one? Aren't they cheaper by the dozen?"

"I'm not making this up," Lily replied, growing angry with her two friends. "Just come with me and see."

"Why should we?" Mozart answered. "You are just going to fool us and then tease us about being suckers and then tell the whole forest about fooling us."

"No, I'm not," Lily continued. "There is, in fact, a real honest-to-goodness angel down by the pond. In fact, it's not just any angel. It's Michael the Angel."

Einstein and Mozart howled with laughter.

"Boy, you always could tell a good story, Lily," Einstein said.

"But it's true!" Lily said. "Every word I'm telling you is true! You must believe me!"

"Okay, then," Mozart replied, "if you are just fooling us, you'll have to give us that big bag of chocolate peanut clusters I spotted hanging in your kitchen yesterday."

"If Michael the Angel is not down by the pond," Lily agreed, "then I will give you the entire bag of chocolate peanut clusters. Every last one of them—every morsel and every crumb will be yours to take."

Now both the owl and the dragon knew Lily rarely shared chocolate peanut clusters with anyone. If the squirrel was willing to part with an entire bag of them over a simple prank, perhaps something was actually happening down by Paula's Pond. If it was merely a prank, they'd still have enough chocolate peanut clusters to eat for a whole month. Either way, they couldn't lose.

"Okay, we will go with you," Einstein said.

Before they would go to the pond, they first made Lily go to her tree and get the sack of chocolate peanut clusters. They wanted the bet paid in full once they got to the shore and found nothing there. Then off they went to the pond, Lily perched on the owl's back as he flew with Mozart clumsily trailing behind them. As they turned at the bend in the path, the moon was rising high in the sky, lighting the area with a pale light. Through the light, they saw something standing on the rock next to the pond.

"I told you!" Lily declared. "See!"

Mozart and Einstein stared into the darkness, their eyes growing larger as they beheld what they saw on the rock. The trio flew toward Michael the Angel who was watching their approach. He was quite an imposing figure, even in the dark. Lily hopped off Einstein's back and onto the rock where Mozart waited. Einstein perched in a tree close to the angel, and the soft glow coming from the angel's wings provided light for them to see.

"My," Mozart said, looking up. "He's certainly a tall one. I bet he's six feet from tip to toe."

"A bit over seven feet," the angel corrected, overhearing the dragon's comment. Michael looked toward Lily. "This is your idea of help, friend squirrel—an owl and a dragon? By the way, has no one ever told you I have this thing about dragons? They kind of creep me out, to be truthful about it."

"This is my friend Mozart the Little Pink Dragon," Lily explained. "And he's a good dragon, quite harmless as a matter of fact. And a bit of a musician as well."

"What about his flame?" the angel asked. "You *do* know those creatures have a tendency to shoot flames at people they don't like?"

"Not much there," Lily answered. Lily turned toward the dragon. "Give Michael a good burp, will you, Mozart?"

Mozart pointed his snout toward the sky and sucked in as much air as he could hold and then let out a belch. With the belch came a tiny pink flame no bigger than the size of a match head. The angel chuckled.

"Well, if that's the best flame this dragon can muster, I guess I'm okay with him."

"Mozart is quite talented musically," Lily said. "Too bad you don't have time to hang around and hear him play his Magical Mushroom Patch. He rocks the house."

Einstein was growing impatient.

"We have come to help you," the owl interrupted, speaking to the tall figure in front of him. "What can we do for you?"

"I've lost my Gold Feather in this pond," Michael explained. "I saw it plop on the surface and then immediately sink. Gold does that, you know. But I don't know exactly where it sank, and it's too dark now to see it. Without it, I'm afraid I can't fly. And if I can't fly, I have failed in my mission and I have failed all the other angels who look to me for guidance. This would not be a good thing."

"We will look for your Gold Feather then," Einstein said enthusiastically. "You have my word we will find it."

That being said, Einstein and Mozart flew over the pond, skimming the surface to see if they could locate the lost feather. They flew back and forth and then forth and back and then back and forth again, but they could find no trace of what they sought. They returned to the rock where Lily and Michael waited.

"It's too dark to see much of anything," Einstein said. "But I will get some more help."

Einstein flew across the pond and located Finnegan and Finagle, the two frogs living in Paula's Pond. He explained the dilemma of the angel and the lost feather. The two frogs plunged headlong into the water and swam across the pond to the rock. They were more curious about getting to see a real angel than to assist with finding a feather but were willing to let circumstance dictate their fate in the matter.

"We will help look for your lost feather," they croaked as they looked up in awe at the huge figure on the rock.

The two frogs leapt back into the water and began to search near the shore, where the water was shallow and the moonbeams lit up the bottom of the pond. They searched for a good bit of time, for there was a great expanse of shallow area near the shoreline. But after a while, they returned to the rock.

"We searched all over the shallow water," Finnegan explained, "but the feather is not there. It must be in deeper water. But it is much too dark to see down there. We will have to wait until the sun rises."

"Oh, no!" Michael exclaimed. "I have to be gone by sunrise! This will not look good on my record if I'm seen in the light of day—not at all good! And I must get this important message to a mother who is worried about her sick child."

"Wait a minute!" Einstein shrieked. "I have an idea. A wonderful and fantastic idea." He patted his shoulder with a wing. "Man, am I a genius or what!"

You see, Einstein had been thinking about the fact that in order to find the Gold Feather lying at the bottom of the pond, more light was needed, and the owl spotted a curious bright glow high in a tree across the water. He flew over to see what the glow was all about, but, in the darkness, he misjudged the distance and instead flew smack into it. To his amazement he found he'd flown into a spider web whose delicate strands shimmered as each reflected the light of the moon back into the sky.

"Hey, you stupid owl!" an irritated female voice shouted. "Look at what you did to my web!"

Einstein was amazed to find the voice coming from a large black spider.

"Sorry," Einstein apologized, "I got too close in the dark."

"I thought you owls were supposed to be wise," the spider scolded. "Look, you fool, you freed my supper."

Einstein watched as a fly buzzed away in the darkness, sticking his tongue out at the spider as it buzzed by his head.

"Just look at that, would you?" the spider fumed. "Thanks to you, my own supper is taunting me. That's embarrassing."

"And just who are you?" Einstein asked.

"I am a spider, naturally," the spider shot back, running two of her legs down the length of her body. "See? And that would explain the web. If you must know, I'm Spinner the Spider. And who would you be?"

"I'm Einstein the Wise Old Owl," he explained, adding a clever comment designed to flatter the spider. "And I must say, I was so taken by the beauty of your web I didn't realize what I was doing. Please forgive me."

"I suppose I will if I will," Spinner answered.

"Yes, that has to be the most beautiful web I have ever seen," Einstein boasted. "Such design, such pattern, such beauty, such intricacy. How in the world did you ever get it to shine so brightly in this darkness?"

"That's secret shimmer shine," Spinner said proudly. "I am the best at making a web shine. It's in my genes."

"Well, Spinner," Einstein began, "how would you like to spin some of your secret shimmer shine for an angel? I mean for a real live honest-to-goodness angel?"

"Stop making fun of me," Spinner cautioned. "Or I will spin the strongest web I've ever spun around you and fasten you to this branch and then not feed you and then invite all my friends over to make fun of you instead."

"I'm not making fun of you," Einstein explained. "Come with me and I'll show you."

Spinner reluctantly crawled on Einstein's beak and clung tightly as the owl lifted his wings and flew across the pond where Mozart, Lily, Michael, and the two frogs waited.

"I have brought help," Einstein said.

"A spider?" the angel answered. "That's your solution, owl? Boy, if I knew we were going to build a zoo, I would have brought Noah with me. He's got more animals in that wooden crate he calls a boat than is in the entire Great Green Forest. What's next, forty days of rain? Or are we going to get busy and find my Gold Feather?"

"Relax, fair angel," Einstein said. "I've got a solid plan in mind."

Einstein put Spinner the Spider on the ground next to the rock.

"We need to find four long sticks," Einstein said.

"Hot dogs—that's great!" Mozart shouted with great excitement. "I'll go get some wieners!" Mozart loved showing off by cooking wieners with the little dragon flame spewing from his snout.

"We're not cooking wieners!" Einstein shouted with annoyance. "Just stop thinking about food, and go get me some sticks. And be quick about it."

81

Mozart and Lily ran into the forest and brought back the sticks the owl requested. They clamored back up the rock and laid them down at the angel's feet. "Now make them into a square," the owl ordered.

Mozart and Lily quickly arranged the sticks into a square, and when that was completed, Einstein turned to Spinner.

"Can you tie the corners of these sticks together with your web shimmer?" he asked. "And they need to be real strong ties."

"I have a very strong web shimmer," Spinner bragged as she began spinning her web around the sticks. "Just don't you worry about that, owl."

Spinner spun the first corner and then the second and in a few minutes had all four corners tied together. Einstein held the square up, testing its strength. Satisfied with the results, he continued.

"Now, Spinner," he said, "can you spin a tight web in this square?"

"Really tight?" Spinner asked.

"Really tight," Einstein replied. "Fill the whole square up with your web. I want it so tight water can't even get through. Think trampoline tight."

"You just watch me work, owl," Spinner answered confidently.

Spinner began spinning back and forth across the sticks, spinning her secret spider shimmer shine row after row tightly. It was amazing to watch how fast the shimmer poured from her body and how she spun it into a strong and tight web. She spun up and down, back and forth, spinning, spinning, and spinning while the others watched admiringly. She worked so quickly Mozart grew dizzy watching her and had to sit down for a moment. When Spinner completed her last spin, they applauded her finished work.

"But what will you do with this thing now?" Spinner asked.

"Just you watch," Einstein said, lifting up the spider's creation.

Einstein held the web up to the sky, and the web caught the light of the moon. The light bounced off the web and onto Michael, who basked in the bright light of moonbeams. Einstein, quite pleased with how his idea worked, smiled. Spinner had spun a brilliant mirror with her secret shimmer shine.

"Wow!" Lily exclaimed. "Look at how bright that light is!"

"Exactly," explained Einstein. "Now we can look for the Gold Feather in the deeper water of the pond."

The angel watched as Einstein sent Finnegan and Finagle into the deep water of the pond, while the owl fluttered overhead, holding the mirror Spinner had spun, directing moonbeams from the face of the mirror into the deep water. The mirror acted like a giant flashlight, its rays cutting into the depths of the lake with ease.

"Wow! Look how bright it is down here now!" Finnegan exclaimed, blowing bubbles of excitement to the surface where the words he spoke underwater escaped as the bubbles burst and were carried up to the owl. As the first rays of the sun barely began to show in the east, Finnegan and Finagle broke through the surface of the pond.

"Hey, look at what I found!" Finnegan declared, breaking the surface of the water.

"Have you found it?" Lily shouted from the bank.

"I found this neat clam shell!" Finnegan yelled back, proudly holding up the white object he discovered. "It will make a neat soap dish."

"Hey, you stupid frog!" Lily shouted. "You're supposed to be looking for a Gold Feather! Now drop that worthless clam shell and get back down there!" She pointed toward the eastern skyline. "And hurry up! The sun is coming up!"

"You wouldn't say that if there was a pearl in there," Finnegan argued.

"Lots of luck finding a pearl in a clam," Lily shot back. "If you want a pearl, go find an oyster. Now get back down there and find that feather."

"Please hurry, friends," the angel begged. Lily saw urgency in the angel's eyes. "Time is growing short."

Finnegan reluctantly did as Lily asked, and a few minutes later, the two frogs emerged from the deep water of the pond once more.

"We've got it!" they declared. "We've got the Gold Feather!"

Michael the Angel watched the first rays of the sun peek over the horizon.

"Please hurry!" he pleaded. "Please, please hurry, friends of the forest!"

Finnegan and Finagle headed toward the shore, the feather held jointly in their mouths as they swam furiously side by side. They were still far out in the pond when Einstein swooped down and plucked the Gold Feather from their mouths. He flew to the rock and turned his head toward Lily who took the prize from his beak.

"Hurry, Lily," Michael pleaded again. "Please hurry."

Lily peeked into the hole in the angel's wing where the feather was to go. She knew something had to be done fast or the dawn would break and the angel would be exposed to the world.

"Spinner, give me some of that secret shimmer shine," Lily instructed, climbing from the wing. "Hurry."

Spinner quickly spun some sticky shimmer shine on Lily's white paw and Lily scurried back up Michael's wing, Gold Feather in one paw and spider shimmer shine in the other. As the sun crept up just a little more, Lily jammed the secret shimmer shine into the hole the feather had fallen from and stuck the Gold Feather back where it was supposed to be. She tried to shake the feather loose but it held firm in the hole.

"That should do it," Lily said happily, scurrying back onto the rock. She gave the angel a thumbs up, smiling as she did so. "I think you're good to go."

Michael the Angel gently flapped his wing a few times and smiled.

"It's fixed!" he exclaimed. "Oh, joy, joy, and joy."

"You must hurry, Michael!" Lily said. "The sun is starting to rise."

"Now I must find that mother," Michael said, "and let her know her child will get well. I must do it quickly."

The angel flapped his wings harder and looked down at the animals, a radiant smile on his face.

"I'll be sure to put in a good word about you to the guys upstairs," he said. And then he added, "Noah would be pretty proud of all of you guys if you ever happened to ride on that old crate of his. The word is he's building a newer model soon though. Why he would do that is beyond me."

"Well, that's just great," Mozart said, adding almost as an after-thought, "hot dogs for breakfast, anyone?"

Then the animals assembled at the rock beheld a most wonderful sight. As the first faint rays of dawn crept from behind the trees, Michael the Angel gracefully lifted his wings and flew above them, soft glowing lights of blue and pink pulsating from beneath his feathers as he passed over the group. He circled the pond once, his white robe flowing in the breeze. He waved down to them and then disappeared into a cloud that had appeared seemingly out of nowhere and then went on his way to give a message of great joy to a worried mother.

Her child would get well.

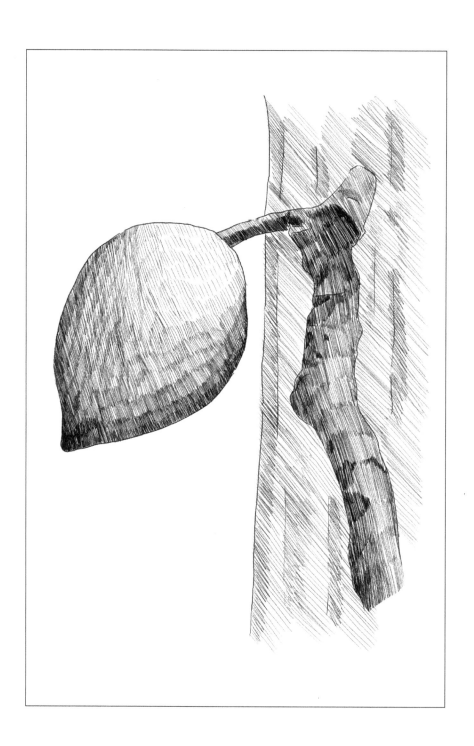

CHAPTER 10

INSIDE LILY'S BUTTERNUT

Now I know this is hard to believe, particularly in the Great Green Forest, but one day, Lily had what one would call a *not-such-a-good day*. Mind you, her day started out very well because just before she woke up that morning, she dreamed she was lolling around quite contently upon a humongous pile of chocolate peanut clusters. She was so happy she began to roll back and forth over the top of the pile of delicious delicacies. In reality, she was sleeping very soundly beneath her quilt, which was filled with warm pink soft flamingo feathers the squirrel had collected over some time from the shore of Paula's Pond. The feathers floated in the water after falling off some local flamingoes that swam near there. As she dreamed, Lily began to roll over the mattress, and pretty soon she rolled over the edge of the bed and banged hard onto the floor below. As you know, falling off one's bed really smarts when the floor smacks into one's face, and it did for Lily, too. Her dream escaped in the blink of a gnat's eye through Lily's ear, and as Lily opened her eyes, she watched her dream flutter through her little oak window and fly away through the trees on a summer breeze.

Now Lily was anxious to see where her dream was heading and thinking maybe it would lead her to the Secret Den of Dreams—that place where dreams go after being dreamed by the dreamer. Lily quickly followed her dream outside. She opened her front door, which proved to be a bit of a mistake, for you see, Lily was not quite awake yet. As she stepped forward along the thick branch just below her front door, her little leg happened to slip on some of the deep green moss carpeting the branch during certain months. Lily lost her balance and tumbled over the side. The little squirrel watched in horror as the ground seemed to shoot up toward her, but just as she was about to ram into the forest floor, she spied a low-hanging branch newly sprung from the main trunk of the giant oak. As her head passed the branch, Lily reached out and grabbed it just as her tail touched the ground. She stopped so fast her vision blurred, and her eyes rolled around and around inside her head, and she felt as though her little arms might be ripped right out of their socket. Her little white whiskers shook and shook but slowly stopped. Luckily, she wasn't very heavy, and everything seemed to still be in place.

As Lily focused her blue eyes, a voice cried out.

"Hey, get off me!" the voice blurted in a very irritated tone. "Get off me!"

Quite startled by the voice, Lily turned her head to her left and saw a huge nose right in front of her face. "Egad!" Lily shouted, quite frightened by the huge nose dwarfing her face.

"Get off me!" yelled the voice behind the huge nose. "You're hurting me."

Lily looked above her to see she was not actually hanging from a tree branch as she had thought, but her little paws clung tightly to the velvety antlers of her friend Robert the Moose. Lily was so surprised by this she let go and thudded gently to the ground.

"Ouch!" Robert said, raising his head but trying to quiet his voice, "Ouch, ouch, ouch."

Robert shook his head and stared down at Lily, a look of disgust on his face.

"Lily, why did you jump on my antlers from so high in the tree?" he asked in a not-at-all happy voice. "Don't you know I just got that kink straightened out from the last adventure we went on?"

Lily looked up at her giant moose friend and tried to explain, remembering not too long ago when both of them were stuck in a bush with

Lily's foot wedged in Robert's ear. It had taken quite a bit of work from some of their friends to get her foot freed. The memory of that fiasco was fresh on the moose's mind.

"I didn't do it on purpose," she explained. "I was in my bed dreaming, and then I fell out and I saw my dream escaping through a window. When I went outside to see where it went, I slipped on some moss and fell from the tree. Just as I was about to hit the ground, I saw a branch and grabbed it. But it wasn't a branch. It was your antlers. So sorry, Robert."

"My beautiful antlers!" Robert huffed. "You thought my beautiful velvet-lined antlers were ordinary tree branches! Well, I never have been so insulted in all my life! Do I look like a tree to you?" The moose snorted. "I believe from now on I will get my grass somewhere else other than from below your tree!"

With that Robert turned his head and stalked briskly away. Lily turned sadly away from the moose and scurried back to the base of the Big Oak. As she did, she stubbed her little toe on a small thistle, and the needle poked into her tender skin.

"Ouch, ouch, and double ouch!" she said as she hopped on one foot around the trunk of the oak. Lily sat down and hung her head. She had been awake for such a very short time, and already the day was going very badly for her. She hoped things would improve as the day went on.

"Woe is me," she moaned, rubbing her little toe. "Woe is me. I lost my best dream ever. Then I fell out of bed. Then I fell off a tree branch. Then I hurt my friend Robert the Moose when I yanked his antlers. Now he is mad at me for thinking his beautiful velvet-lined antlers were tree branches. And now I stubbed by toe. Woe is me. Whatever will happen next?"

Lily looked around the forest and saw other animals were now watching her. *They are laughing at me*, she thought. But she was wrong. They weren't laughing at her. You see, they were all her friends, and friends don't laugh when other friends are hurt. But Lily was having such a bad day she didn't stop to consider this. She decided she would run away and be by herself for a while and no one would find her. Lily stood up and turned her back on the forest animals she so dearly loved but sometimes did not appreciate. She began to walk along a well-worn path in the woods.

Lily walked and walked, and then she walked some more. She walked such a long way she didn't realize this part of the Great Green Forest was unfamiliar to her. She was deep in thought and barely paid any attention to just how far she had walked or how long she had been walking. Finally, she came to a fork in the path. *Funny*, she thought. *I don't remember this fork being here.* If she thought about it, she might realize she'd never been to this part of the Great Green Forest, and she wouldn't have recognized this particular fork anyway. Lily noticed the left fork led into an opening in the bushes, but beyond where the bushes grew, she couldn't see what was up the path. The right fork led to an open clearing, and she could see nothing appearing to be dangerous there.

As a curious squirrel will do, Lily chose the path leading into the bushes. As she walked along the path and drew closer to the bushes, she still could see nothing beyond them but darkness. Lily stopped and hesitated, afraid to enter. She peered into an opening in the branches and spied what appeared to be a huge room made of bushes, almost like a green cave. As curious squirrels must do, Lily thought she would take one brave step inside to remind herself she was still brave, twitch her tail back and forth a couple of times just to be cool, and then quickly scurry back out onto the path and safety.

That is just what Lily did. She took one step inside the large green cave of bushes, twitched her long white tail, and then turned to leave, content with the state of her bravery. However, as she turned, the hole in the bushes began to close, trapping her inside the green cave. It grew so dark even Lily's shadow deserted her, scampering up the path just as the bushes closed behind. A piece of the shadow ripped off and hung on the bushes just outside where the opening had once been. Alone in the darkness, Lily began to tremble while her shadow waited outside, wondering if there was a seamstress or a knitter or even a sail-stitcher nearby who could repair the tear in a shadow.

"Fear not, Lily," a soothing voice said in the darkness. "I won't hurt you."

"Who's there? Who are you?" Lily answered, sensing a soothing voice must be a friendly voice and a voice that could help her. She stopped trembling.

"It's me, Lily," the mysterious voice answered once more. "I am the Wise Wizard of the Great Green Forest."

"The Forest Wizard?" Lily scoffed. "Give me a break! How do I know who you are? You could be anybody in the dark and just trying to get my goat."

"I don't want your goat," the voice shot back, "or anybody else's goat for that matter. I could easily conjure up a goat if I really wanted one. Ever seen a polka-dotted goat or a goat with a furry green coat? Why, I could snap my fingers and make one. That's child's play. But I find goats rather repulsive and smelly in fact. They could all use a good dousing of fragrant French perfume."

"That's just a saying, whoever you are," Lily defended. "Getting my goat means you're trying to put one over on me. And let me tell you right now, I'm much too smart for that."

"Didn't your mother ever tell you about me?" the voice asked. "Didn't she tell you about the Forest Wizard of the Great Green Forest?"

"Yes, I do believe she did mention a Forest Wizard of the Great Green Forest maybe once or twice," Lily replied. "But that was when she was telling me bedtime tales. I always thought she just made you up. You know how moms are. They'd tell you anything to get you to go to sleep at night."

"Your mother didn't make that story up, Lily," the voice in the darkness explained. "She needed help once, so I helped her."

"Who is out there talking to me?" Lily asked. "Who is playing this trick on me? Don't you know how bad my day has been already?"

To her amazement Lily watched as the green cave of bushes slowly lit up. As it did, there before her, in a purple satin robe, stood the Forest Wizard. He wore a pointy purple hat that reminded Lily of a pointy hat her mother once made for her as a learning tool when all other methods of teaching failed. She had only been allowed to wear it when she sat on a stool in a corner, facing the wall. Lily hadn't liked either the lesson taught or the tool used to teach the lesson, but she also remembered her mother never needed to teach her that lesson again. If her mother was forced to use an unusual procedure to get her point across, Lily reminded herself, then she must have thought her method was worth the effort. Lily was grateful. She remembered her mother fondly and her heart skipped a beat. She missed her dearly.

"Well, Lily," he said. "Do you believe your mother now?"

Lily was speechless as she heard his words. Flecks of gold on the wizard's flowing robe shone light on Lily's white fur, and bits of light bounced from her blue eyes and little white nose to dance before the wizard. She looked at the top of his pointed hat and saw a gold ball made of short, fuzzy tassels that jiggled whenever he moved his head. Lily felt a calm feeling come over her, and all the thoughts of her bad day began to disappear. Even her injured foot ceased throbbing.

"I know all about your bad day, Lily," the Forest Wizard explained. "I know about your lost dream. I know you fell out of bed. I know you fell from your tree. I know you hung from the antlers of Robert the Moose and you accidentally hurt his feelings. And I know you stubbed your poor little toe and then ran away from your friends. I know all these things."

"Woe is me," Lily moaned, recalling all that had happened to her. "Why did you have to bring all those bad memories back up? Now I feel even worse than I did a minute ago. Woe is me."

"Lily," the Forest Wizard explained, "I must remind you of all those things for one very important reason. That's because I have your butternut."

"You have my what?" Lily asked, not believing what she was hearing.

The Wise Wizard held open his hand. In it was a wrinkled, oblong object made of wood. It was, indeed, a butternut, just a plain ordinary old brown butternut like hundreds and hundreds of others scattered on the forest floor.

"Your butternut," he said pointing. "This one is yours."

Lily was dumbfounded.

"My butternut!" she exclaimed, staring at the wizard's hand and then into his face. "There are lots of butternuts in the woods. How do you know that one is mine? Why would I need my own butternut?" She pointed to the wizard's hand. "And what could be in that one butternut that would make it any different than any other butternut laying around in the Great Green Forest?"

Lily was beginning to seriously think the Forest Wizard might actually be off his own nut. She learned that saying from her mother who used it on her sometimes when, as a young squirrel, she did something goofy.

"You certainly are a lot like your mother, Lily," he said. "But I can assure you this particular butternut is yours. That's one great advantage to being a wizard, my little squirrel friend. We get to know stuff just because we get to know stuff. But tell me, Lily, what do you think is inside of this butternut?"

"It's nutmeat, of course," Lily shot back. "It's the same stuff you find inside of *any* nut." She stared at him. "Are you sure you're a wizard?"

"Yes, Lily," he replied, smiling down at her. "I am a Wizard First Class, as a matter of fact, certified by the Worldwide Ones Who Watch, or WOWW for short. But let's return to my original question, Lily. Since this is your butternut, and yours alone, are you absolutely sure nutmeat and only nutmeat is what's inside it?"

Lily thought about that for a moment.

"I know that nutmeat is all that's supposed to be in there," she replied rather unsure of her answer. "That's certainly true for any nut."

"Don't be fooled by what you have been told of what might be in there or what you think should be in there, Lily. Remember, this is your butternut. Let me ask you this then. What do you want to be in your butternut?"

Lily thought long and hard about what the wizard asked. Now she was really confused.

"Well," she finally replied, "if it's not nutmeat in there, whatever is there would have to be something pretty small but important, I suppose. I can't think of anything I would want that would fit inside of a butternut shell except a butternut. The nutmeat is so good."

"Why couldn't something bigger be in there?" the Forest Wizard asked.

"Because it wouldn't fit," Lily explained. "Are you absolutely sure you're a wizard?"

"You wouldn't believe how many times I get asked that question," the Forest Wizard replied. "I always have to answer 'yes' even to the most skeptical. That always gets their goat as well."

"Well," Lily said. "You shouldn't be so surprised people ask that question. I mean, some of the things you are telling me are most, let's say, unbelievable."

"It's good you find me interesting," the Forest Wizard smiled. "But, back to my question again. What do you think is inside of your butternut? Or perhaps I should pose the question another way. What do you want to be inside of your butternut, Lily, if you had a choice that is?"

Lily mulled his words for a moment before speaking.

"Something like me," she answered. "Something that is me. Or perhaps even something that will be me?" Lily didn't know why she said what she did next, but she blurted it out. "We get to say stuff just because we say stuff." Then, thinking about her last remark, she added, "Oh, maybe I shouldn't have said that."

"You are, indeed, much like your mother," the Forest Wizard said. "You see, Lily, when it comes right down to it, the same things you wish were inside of the butternut are the same things inside you." He pointed to her heart. "Inside you, my friend, there is beauty, and there will be beauty inside of your butternut. It doesn't matter whether you can see it or not. It just matters that you believe it's there. It doesn't matter, Lily, if you have one bad day where you think everything has gone wrong in your world. How you live your own life and how you treat your friends will ultimately determine what will be inside your butternut. The important stuff inside your butternut will not be determined by falling out of a tree, or hanging from a moose's antlers, or even from stubbing your toe. When you exist, both joy and sorrow will find you, and that's just the way it is and always will be."

Lily listened intently to the words of the Forest Wizard and then asked him a question.

"When will I know what's inside of my butternut, Great Wizard?"

He smiled down at her and spoke.

"Why don't you just let me be concerned about that for now, Lily, and don't worry your furry little head about it?" He looked around. "It is just about time for you to go, anyway." Then he added something. "By the way, you're always adding stuff to your butternut, Lily. Don't ever forget that. Take care with what you do."

The Forest Wizard pointed to the bushes, and Lily saw the opening appear once more. As she turned to say goodbye, Lily saw the Forest Wizard vanish into thin air. *Now you're just showing off*, Lily thought. She turned away and walked through the hole in the bushes, stopping to pick the torn piece of her shadow from one of the branches.

"Here, you dropped this," she said, as her shadow ran down the path to greet her.

As she walked back to the main path, Lily glanced back to see the hole in the bushes closed and the path that had led there slowly disappear. She handed the dark torn piece back to her shadow and watched as it scurried up the path ahead of her with the torn piece firmly clutched in one hand. No doubt her shadow was heading lickety-split to find a seamstress, or a knitter, or maybe even a sail-stitcher to sew the torn piece back on and then get back to the business of being a full-blown shadow in good standing with the shadow community once more and whose proficiency at mimicking its owner's moves was second to none. Later that day Lily found her friend Robert the Moose, and the two played for the rest of the day, neither bringing up the earlier incident of Lily landing on the moose's antler.

And once in a while, Lily thought about her butternut and hoped that when the time came to open it, whenever that time should come, she would be pleasantly surprised by what she found inside.

CHAPTER 11

LILY AND SAM THE MAILMAN

Every day, Monday through Saturday, Sam the Mailman came to the Great Green Forest to deliver the mail. Other than Freddie the Indian, who lived in the forest, Sam was about the only human the forest animals ever saw. Sam was reluctant at first to enter a place where a bear or a moose or some other sort of creature might pop out and bite him or suck on his ear or sting his bulbous nose or even pluck out some of his curly hair with which to build a nest. When he'd brought up his fear of the forest to his supervisor, however, he'd been severely reproached.

"Now see here, my good fellow," the supervisor, a former resident of England who'd moved across the ocean on a whim, gotten a job with the Post Office, and climbed the ranks to supervisor, said, "You know our motto, Sam. 'Neither snow nor rain nor heat nor gloom of night keeps our couriers from delivering all that's right.'" Then he added something that may or may not have been printed in the official Post Office Book of Rules he read from, but he pretended to read from it anyway. "And whatever creature might pop out and bite you or suck on your ear or sting your bulbous nose or might even pluck out some of your curly hair to build a nest still deserves to get mail from their loved ones." He stared at Sam to make sure his point was made. "Remember, Sam, everyone has a loved one somewhere. They all deserve to get their mail delivered, regardless of where they live. Even Eskimos get mail, and they live in igloos in quite far off and very cold places."

It never occurred to Sam that some poor fellow mail carrier had to fight his way through blinding snowstorms to deliver mail to a lonely Eskimo who was probably having to eat icicles and whale blubber for breakfast while living in an igloo built on some remote iceberg bobbing up and down in a freezing sea by the North Pole. And to add to his dilemma, the poor Eskimo might only have white walls inside his home and never get to paint them neat colors like other people get to do. Pondering the trials of the Eskimo mailman, Sam considered himself lucky and never again brought up his reluctance to enter the Great Green Forest. With the exception of losing some hair to a farsighted crow frantically trying to collect supplies to build an emergency bird nest, Sam was never bothered by any creature of the forest. He was occasionally rewarded when a chocolate peanut cluster would suddenly and mysteriously drop into his mail sack when he walked under a particularly large oak tree with an itty-bitty door high in its branches.

Sam brought mail to Einstein the Wise Old Owl, Mozart the Little Pink Dragon, Elvis the Toucan Bird, and Freddie the Indian, as well as everyone else who lived in the Great Green Forest. After a while Sam didn't have to even look at the addresses on some of the mail. He knew certain animals received certain kinds of mail during certain times, and often he didn't even have to look at the name on the envelope. He'd just stick it in a mailbox or under the rump of a sleeping Elvis as he snored away in his nest or leave a letter dangling from Spinner the Spider's web or resting on a rock for the frogs Finnegan and Finagle to find. He'd even pranked Freddie the Indian once by leaving a plastic bottle of Heavenly Rain Dance Water tucked inside the Indian's loincloth. When poor Freddie rolled over on his belly as he slept, the lid of the bottle came off, and when Freddie woke up, he thought he accidently wet himself during his nap. When Freddie mentioned that little mishap to Sam later, the mailman promised to leave the Heavenly Rain Dance Water just outside Freddie's tent from then on.

Sam knew Redfriend the Skunk received his monthly issue of Perfume Illustrated on the third day of every month, and Einstein the

Wise Old Owl couldn't wait to get his wings on his copy of Really Weird Science Quarterly. Mozart the Little Pink Dragon anxiously waited to read Dragon Lover's Digest, a quite thick bimonthly magazine in which Mozart was once featured playing the Hokey Pokey on his Magical Mushroom Patch, probably the first time in history that melody had been played in its entirely on a set of magical mushroom drums.

Now one cool morning, Lily sat on the branch high in the tree and watched the mailman as he completed his mail route. *That guy sure doesn't smile much*, Lily thought as she watched Sam put a letter in her mailbox on the trunk of the Big Oak. Then a brilliant idea came to her. She would play a trick on the mailman, and he would laugh so hard he would probably drop his sack of mail right on his foot because he was shaking so uncontrollably.

Bright and early the next morning, while all the other animals were still sleeping, Lily crept very quietly down the trunk of the Big Oak and crawled inside of the mailbox and closed the door. Then she sat down in the dark to wait for Sam to come strolling along. When the mailman opened the door to put the mail in, Lily planned to jump out and scare him and then they both would have a big laugh at how clever Lily was to think of a trick like this. But most importantly, she would finally get Sam the Mailman to smile, for someone who's not happy at his job is not a happy someone.

The sun peeked up over the top of the trees as the rest of the forest animals began to wake up. But none of them knew Lily was hiding in the mailbox waiting to play a trick on Sam the Mailman. Everyone began to wonder where the little squirrel was, but nobody could find their beloved Lily. The sun rose high above the treetops and began to shine down on the mailbox. The sun's rays warmed the mailbox, and inside, where Lily was hiding, it was soon toasty warm. It grew so warm Lily became tired.

"Perhaps I will take a little nap," Lily said to herself. "That is what I will do. Then I will wake up just in time to surprise Sam the Mailman when he opens the door."

Lily nestled down contently in a ball of soft white fur and was soon fast asleep inside the mailbox. She slept while all around her the animals of the forest played. She slept while the sun climbed even higher into the morning sky. In fact, Lily was still sleeping when Sam the Mailman walked along the path with his sack of mail. Sam opened the mailbox to put the mail inside, just like he did every other day, but found something was already in the mailbox. Something very white and very furry— something very white and very furry and very much asleep was curled up inside the mailbox. Sam the Mailman quietly shut the door.

"Why, I bet that darn squirrel was waiting inside that mailbox just so she could jump out and scare me," Sam declared.Then he thought for a minute.

"I'll teach that scoundrel to try and outsmart me, that I will," Sam whispered, looking at the name on the mailbox. "I will play a trick on Lily instead."

Sam the Mailman reached into his mail sack and pulled out an empty box. Then as quietly as possible, he opened the door to the mailbox and reached inside. He gently picked up Lily and pulled her out of the mailbox. Can you guess what he did then? He licked a stamp and put it right between Lily's ears, all the time snickering about how funny it was that instead of Lily playing a trick on him, he was going to play a trick on Lily. Then he took a little vial of sleeping powder from his shirt pocket and sprinkled some powder on Lily's little white nose. This was a yellow dust he took when he couldn't sleep at night. As he watched Lily sniff in her sleep, he knew the little squirrel wouldn't be waking up anytime soon. He gently put Lily inside of the box and taped the box shut. Sam put more stamps on the outside of the box—lots and lots of stamps. Then he pulled out a big magic marker pen and wrote on the box where he was going to send it. He chuckled as he wrote in big letters:

To: *The President of the Whole United States of America The House Where the Big Dude Lives, Washington, DC*

He carefully slid the box into his mail sack and continued on his way delivering the mail.

Deep inside the warmth of the dark box, Lily continued to sleep. Lily slept when Sam the Mailman arrived back at the Post Office and dropped the box into a big sack that read "Out of Town Mail." Lily was still sleeping as the big sack was loaded into a truck and taken to the airport and put on a plane. Lily was still asleep when the plane landed at the airport in Washington, DC, early the next morning. Lily was finally jolted awake when the box was abruptly dropped down on something quite hard. Now Lily had no idea she slept so long or that Sam the Mailman found her and gave her a little something to keep her sleeping. She'd never slept so long in her life and had no idea just how long her sleep lasted. She thought she was still inside of the mailbox back in the Great Green Forest. Lily was ready to jump out and scare Sam with a big "Boo!" when the door opened. When the top of the box finally opened, that's just what she did. She jumped out and yelled out "Boo!" just as loud as her little squirrel voice would let her.

However, as she jumped out, she found she was not in her forest of leafy trees with Sam the Mailman, but instead she found she was in the Oval Office of the White House of the Capital of the Entire Government of the Whole United States of America in Washington, DC. In front of her stood not Sam the Mailman, whom she expected, but the President of the Whole United States of America. The President jumped backward with fright, his hand on his chest, because Lily popped out of the box and scared him dreadfully. You see, it was the President's birthday, and the President thought he was just opening a birthday present from some admirer. Imagine his surprise when a white squirrel with a postage stamp stuck between her ears jumped out shouting, "Boo!" Wouldn't you be just a little scared, too?

Two burly guards immediately grabbed Lily, holding on tightly to her little arms. They were about to take her off to jail until the President called them back.

"Wait," the President said, "let us not be too hasty in our judgment."

Then the President spoke to Lily.

"Why did you want to scare me, Little Squirrel?" he asked.

"My name is Lily, Sir," Lily answered, sounding quite frightened, which, indeed, she was. She could see the Presidential Seal on his desk and knew the man wielded great power. She began speaking fast to the President, her voice cracking.

"I don't know what I'm doing here, oh mighty President. I was in my mailbox in the Great Green Forest is all I remember. I was going to trick Sam the Mailman by scaring him and maybe get him to smile—he doesn't do that much—and instead I fell asleep. I woke up just now and jumped out of the box when the lid opened, and I scared you instead, oh mighty President. I'm sorry I ever tried to trick anybody. Now I'm going to jail, and I may never see my forest or my friends or even my mailman again."

"It would be very sad for something to happen to a fine-looking animal such as you, Lily," the President chuckled, as he gently pulled the stamp from the squirrel's forehead. "For I know you were only trying to play a joke on your mail carrier. I'll tell you what. Why don't you stay with me today and help me celebrate my birthday? We'll have some fun, okay? Then we'll make sure you get back home safely. Would that be okay?"

"Oh, thank you Mr. President of the Whole United States," Lily said. "That would be very nice. I would surely like to have some fun with you in your wonderful big house."

For the rest of the day, Lily hung out with the President of the Whole United States, playing games and eating chocolate peanut clusters. Lily kept winning at hide-and-seek because she would crawl up the wall and hide on the chandeliers next to the ceiling, and no one was able to find her there because Lily was as white as the ceiling and almost invisible to anyone looking for her. Lily and the President played for six hours until Lily became very tired and fell asleep on the big desk in the Oval Office. Her adventure had completely exhausted her, and her little squirrel belly was chock-full of chocolate peanut clusters. She fell into a deep slumber and even snored, which made the President chuckle, though softly so as not to wake her. The President got a box and put Lily in it. Then he took Lily's little paw and stamped something on it with a metal seal. He closed the box up and got a big black magic marker and wrote on the front of the box:

To: *Sam the Mailman*
The Great Green Forest, USA

Lily was exhausted from the events of the day. She slept soundly when the President slid the box into the White House mail sack marked "Out of Town Mail." Lily slept as the mail sack was loaded onto a truck and driven to the airport. Lily was still sleeping when the plane landed the next morning. It was only when the box was set down abruptly that Lily finally woke up. The top of the box opened and Lily peered up, and guess what she saw? That's right—it was Sam the Mailman who opened the box!

"What is this?" Sam asked, amazed at seeing Lily sitting inside of the box.

"It's me, Sam!" Lily answered. "I have returned from seeing the President of the Whole United States of America, thanks to you."

"Oh come now, Lily," Sam the Mailman replied. "Are you trying to tell me you met the President of the Whole United States?"

"Not only did I meet him," Lily replied, "but I spent all day with him on his birthday. We played games and ate chocolate peanut clusters and had all sorts of fun. Then I got so tired I just had to sleep, and he must have mailed me back to you."

"Now wait," Sam cut in as Lily's forest friends began gathering around them to listen. "Do you really think we are foolish enough to believe a story so wild?"

"It's true," Lily defended, raising her paw as if she were taking an oath. "Every word I have told you is the truth. I swear it."

Lily's friends began laughing at her.

"She really expects us to believe that," Sam said.

"Well, who cares what you think," Lily replied, angry with her friends for not believing her story. "I'm going home."

Now, Elvis the Toucan Bird, who, by the way, is a very observant bird, had noticed something on Lily's paw.

"Wait!" he shouted over the laughter. "Lily is telling the truth about what she did."

The animals began to laugh once more, this time at Elvis. But Elvis held up one of his wings and motioned for them to be silent.

"I can prove Lily has been to Washington and has seen the President of the Whole United States," Elvis declared.

Elvis took the paw Lily had held up and turned it over in his wing.

"Look," he instructed, pointing down at Lily's palm. "Look here."

Sam the Mailman and all the animals looked at Lily and were very surprised as they read what was stamped on her palm. In big blue letters, the President had put his seal, and all the animals saw the words, "THE OFFICE OF THE PRESIDENT OF THE WHOLE UNITED STATES OF AMERICA" stamped right on Lily's paw. They knew the only way Lily could have gotten that stamp was by being in the Oval Office of the White House of the Capital of the Entire Government of the Whole United States of America in Washington, DC.

"You really did see the President," the animals said with admiration. "Good for you."

"Yes," Lily beamed with pride. "Yes I did."

Can you imagine what happened then? For the first time in Lily's memory, Sam the Mailman smiled at her. It seemed to Lily that Sam's smile was probably the biggest one she had ever seen in all her little squirrel life. Of course, Lily was smart enough to know that when you get a smile, you give back a smile. She smiled back at Sam with her brightest smile she saved just for special occasions such as this. Then for the rest of the day, Lily sat with her friends telling of the day she spent at the White House eating chocolate peanut clusters and playing hide-and-seek with the President of the Whole United States on his birthday.

CHAPTER 12

LILY FOOLS FREDDIE THE INDIAN

One bright spring day, Lily was walking with her Little Pink Dragon friend Mozart along one of the many paths in the Great Green Forest that led to Paula's Pond. As usual, Mozart, who liked music, was tapping a stick on just about everything they would walk by. You see, Mozart thought everything had at least one good musical note buried somewhere inside of it, and the little dragon was forever trying to get those notes to come out so they could be enjoyed by everyone who happened to be around to hear them. Once in a while, as the squirrel and the dragon walked along, Lily would glance over at her friend who was banging a stick on everything they passed.

"Don't you ever get tired of doing that?" Lily asked, somewhat annoyed.

For you see, although Mozart was her friend, it sometimes drove Lily crazy when the dragon banged on everything within reach of his tiny claws.

"Not really," Mozart said. "I'm just trying to find the hidden notes in all of these things." The dragon banged on a tree trunk as they passed by, and a dull thud escaped from it. "See, listen to that sweet sound, my little squirrel friend. There are many other great things to bang on. There's just not enough time in the day to whack on them all."

Then he tapped a large rock and they heard a sound.

"You see," Mozart said, "listen to that sound. There is music in this rock. That's a 'bricky-brack' note—sounds like someone hitting a brick."

Now Lily appreciated music, but not as much as Mozart. She was tired of all his tapping and banging as they walked along. *I mean, enough is enough*, the squirrel thought.

"May I see your stick?" she asked, holding out her little white paw.

Mozart held out the stick.

"Oh, do you think you can find a musical note in something?" he asked.

"I can try," Lily answered.

With that, Lily took the stick and rapped the top of Mozart's head several times, beating out a dull tap-tap-tap sound.

"Oh," she said, pretending to be amazed, "just listen to that sound. Such a sweet sound! Sweet but hollow, I might add."

Lily secretly hoped she had pounded some sense into her little friend's head and that he would now have the sense not to pound on *everything*. Mozart didn't know exactly what to think of this strange thing the squirrel had just done to his head. But he knew his brain was pounding and logically concluded that this must be what a drum felt like after a concert.

"Well," he said, taking the stick back from Lily while rubbing the top of his head, "perhaps we should just walk to the pond and see who's there this morning."

"Good idea, indeed," Lily answered, quite pleased with herself for stopping the annoying racket the dragon had been making during their journey.

The squirrel and the little dragon continued along the path leading to the pond. Lily found the quiet very relaxing and glanced over to her friend who had seemed to calm down a bit. They emerged from the trees and found themselves on a hill overlooking the calm waters of the pond. Down below them, sleeping quite comfortably on his back, with his hands behind his head, was Freddie the Indian. His gangly body stretched out on a blanket, his head resting on a pillow he'd made, his long black hair scattered around his head. Freddie was, in fact, sleeping so soundly they could hear his loud snoring from where they stood.

"Hey!" Lily said. "That's Freddie! Look at that big goof off napping this early in the day."

Lily and Mozart studied the Indian as he slept. After a few moments, the two looked at each other.

"You know, Mozart," Lily said with a mischievous twinkle in her eyes, "Freddie looks like he's just too comfortable down there. You know, we would be doing him a favor if we did something to him. It might let him know he always needs to be on guard here in the forest." She smiled mischievously. "It's for his own good, mind you."

Mozart smiled back at Lily.

"For his own good. You know, Lily, you are right. We need to teach that lazy old Indian a lesson in being aware of one's surroundings."

The two discussed what they might do to the Indian and came up with a brilliant plan. They scurried away to their homes and came back quickly before the Indian woke up. Lily brought a small can of paint and a tiny brush from her house while Mozart brought a stepladder and a small cloth bag stuffed to the brim with something inside. The squirrel and the dragon walked over to where the Indian lay and saw Freddie was still sound asleep and still snoring very loudly. And it didn't appear as though their friend was going to wake up any time soon. Lily picked up some dandelion fluff and placed it over the Indian's mouth. When Freddie snored once more, the fluff blew high into the air and floated away.

"I don't think there's much danger that Freddie will wake up until we are done here," Mozart said as he watched the fluff float out over the pond. He snickered. "Let's get to work then."

Mozart opened his stepladder over Freddie's belly as Lily lifted the lid off the can she had fetched. The can was filled with black paint and Lily dipped the brush tip into the can and handed it to Mozart. The dragon gingerly climbed the stepladder stretched over the Indian like a miniature teepee, watching Freddie's belly rise and fall as he breathed. Lily stood on the bottom rung of the ladder as Mozart leaned over the top step of the ladder and pointed the brush toward Freddie's belly button. Lily snickered as he watched his friend.

"Is this a neat idea or what?" she chuckled. "This is going to drive him nuts."

Mozart was too busy to acknowledge what Lily said. The little dragon was balanced on the top step of the ladder and was trying to wait until just the right moment to stick the paintbrush into Freddie's belly button. As Freddie inhaled in his sleep, his belly dropped, and as it did so, Mozart stuck the brush inside the Indian's belly button and swirled it around. As the Indian breathed out, his belly rose, and Mozart pulled the brush out and handed it to Lily, who stuck the bristles into the can to get more paint. Three more times Mozart stuck the brush into Freddie's belly button until he was satisfied his work was complete. Then he motioned for Lily to join him at the top of the ladder, where the two admired the finished work.

"Oh, I think our Freddie is going to be quite surprised," Lily chuckled, careful not to be too loud and risk waking their friend. "Now, let's be off and let the real fun begin."

You see, the two rascally animals had painted the inside of Freddie's belly button as black as it could be, and they were now planning to trick him. Lily and Mozart sat on the hill overlooking the pond for a while and then, satisfied enough time passed for the paint in Freddie's belly button to dry, continued with the next step of their mischievous plan. Taking the cloth bag with them, they returned to the spot where Freddie slept. Lily opened the bag and looked inside. Within the bag were dozens of buttons, some of which had two holes and some of which had four. There were all shapes and sizes and colors of buttons inside the bag. Lily and Mozart grabbed handfuls of buttons and scattered them all around Freddie's body. When they were through, they hid the bag in the forest.

"Now all we have to do is wait for him to wake up," Mozart chuckled.

"Why wait?" Lily asked. "Let's wake Mr. Lazy Bones up right now."

Lily and Mozart climbed back down the hill and pretended like they were just arriving at the pond. They came out of the forest singing and acted startled when they spotted Freddie as he woke up when he heard their singing.

"Oh," Lily exclaimed, as Freddie sat up, "we are so sorry, friend Freddie. We didn't know you were here or we wouldn't have sung so loudly. How rude of us."

"That's okay, Lily," Freddie answered groggily. He yawned, stretching his arms over his head. "I suppose I have slept long enough anyway."

Freddie stood up and yawned a second time.

"Oh my, Freddie!" Lily shouted, pretending to be quite alarmed as she pointed at his belly. "It appears as though you lost something."

Freddie became more red-faced than usual because he was afraid his loincloth had fallen off and he would be embarrassed. He looked down at his waist and found his loincloth still hanging right where it was supposed to be. Then he felt his head and found his lone eagle feather was still sticking from his headband.

"Quit fooling around, Lily," he scolded. "I haven't lost anything."

"Sure, you haven't," Mozart said knowingly. "Take a peek at your belly."

Freddie looked rather clumsy as he bent over to examine his belly. He bent down and then glanced up at the squirrel and the dragon, thinking they were just teasing him.

"Look at your belly button," Lily said. "Look really close this time."

Freddie looked in the hole where his belly button normally sat and gasped.

"Help!" he shouted. He looked around, his eyes searching the area. "Some scoundrel has stolen my belly button while I slept. Is there no decency left anywhere?"

"Are you sure it's gone?" Lily asked, winking at Mozart.

"Of course, I'm sure, you silly squirrel!" Freddie shouted. "Can't you see there's nothing but a black hole there where my belly button is supposed to be? Some rotten no-good has made off with it. What in the world would someone possibly do with a second belly button?"

"A black hole?" Mozart asked innocently. "Maybe you've always had a black hole there and just didn't notice it until now."

"You goofy dragon," Freddie argued. "Of course, I had a belly button. I've seen my reflection in the water of this pond hundreds of times, and it's always been there. Don't try and tell me I've never had a belly button. I couldn't stomach the thought of it."

"But how do you know someone stole your belly button, Freddie?" Lily asked. "How do you know it just didn't fall off while you slept? After all, you do snore rather loudly, and perhaps you just loosened it and it shot off into the air when you let loose one of those big snores you're famous for."

Freddie pondered what the squirrel said.

"Okay," he said. "That sort of makes sense. After all, nuts fall from trees and berries drop from bushes. It might be that my loud snoring is at the root of my missing belly button. If that's the case, I will look for it. It couldn't have gone far. It has to be right around here somewhere."

He looked down at the ground and discovered the area was littered with colorful buttons.

"Look at all these buttons," he exclaimed. "Egad! What are they doing here? How will I ever know which button is mine?"

Lily and Mozart glanced at each other, grinning.

"I guess you'll just have to try them all," Lily suggested. "That is, until you find your very own belly button. And you can put the ones you have already tried and don't fit into a pile. That way you won't get confused and try some of them twice. By the way, I can't recall. Freddie, is your belly button an innie or an outie?"

"It's an outie," Freddie answered, "if you really must know." He huffed. "Is nothing private anymore?"

Freddie began picking up buttons and placing them over the hole in his stomach, hoping one of them would be his. In all the confusion, the poor Indian couldn't remember exactly what color or size his belly button had been. He was forced to try as many as he could until he felt sure he found the right one. He tried buttons with two holes and the buttons with four holes, placing each flat against his stomach. Some were way too big, and some were way too small, so small he had to dig them out with a twig. He tried lots and lots of colored buttons. He tried different-shaped buttons, but he was sure his belly button had been round, and not triangular or square. Finally, when he placed a rather large green four-holed button against his belly, Lily and Mozart could stand it no longer. The two pranksters ran behind a rock and rolled in the grass, laughing until their sides hurt. Of course, Freddie didn't notice, for he replaced the large green four-holed button with a smaller orange two-holed button that didn't fit either. Finally, he placed the last remaining deep purple-colored button over the hole in his stomach.

"Oh, shucks," he said. "This one doesn't fit, either." He moaned. "I guess I'm never going to get my belly button back."

Lily and Mozart popped up from behind the rock.

"You know," Lily said, "I bet I know what happened to your belly button."

"You do?" Freddie asked. "You think you do?"

Lily looked across the pond and pointed.

"See those two frogs on that lily pad over there," she said. "They are Finnegan and Finagle, and they like to pull pranks. I bet they took your belly button. It would be just like them to do something like that to you. Remember when they took the mushroom caps from Mozart's magical mushroom drums? They probably took your belly button and threw it into the pond."

"Threw my belly button in the pond!" Freddie shouted, shaking his fist at the frogs. "I'll get you for this! I will! I will! I will! I will fry your skinny frog legs for my dinner!"

The two frogs looked over at the Indian, wondering why their friend was so upset and why he would shake his fist at them. They both let out a loud croak at the Indian and resumed their lily pad floating.

"See, look at them grinning over there," Lily said, pointing. "They think they're funny. They probably threw your belly button right near the water's edge for we all know frogs are lazy by nature and wouldn't be bothered carrying anything very far."

"I'll look there then," Freddie answered. "And when I find my belly button, I will catch those blasted frogs. Then I'll tie them up with their own legs, and they can see how funny they think that is."

Freddie waded into the shallow water of the pond and looked around the clear water for his missing belly button. He waded in until the water was up to his chest, and when he did so, an amazing thing happened. As Freddie moved, he disturbed the pond water, and the moving water began to wash the black paint from his belly button. High in the sky above, Einstein the Wise Old Owl saw Freddie in the water and then spotted Lily and Mozart on the bank. He sensed there was mischief afoot, and he didn't want to miss out on it. The owl flew to the branch of a nearby tree to observe what was going on.

Lily and Mozart howled with laughter as Freddie searched the bottom of the pond for his lost belly button. Lily laughed so hard she fell off a rock. Freddie searched for a rather long time but could not find his lost belly button. He turned and headed back toward the bank, casting a nasty look at the frogs as he shook his fist at them. As he emerged from the water, Freddie didn't realize all of the paint had washed from his skin. His belly button shined brightly in the sunlight because even the belly button lint collecting there for months had been washed away. As his feet touched the dry bank, he threw his hands into the air.

"I'll never find my belly button!" he cried. "It is lost forever! Woe is me! Woe is me! I am forced to roam the earth like this."

Freddie was unaware Einstein was watching from a tree branch nearby. The owl shook his head as if disgusted by the Indian's behavior.

"Now just what's the matter with you, Freddie?" the owl asked. "What's all this nonsense about a missing belly button?"

Lily and Mozart heard Einstein talking to Freddie and rolled on the ground, laughing harder.

"My belly button," Freddie explained to the owl, "it's missing. I'll never be a complete Indian anymore."

Einstein stared at Freddie's belly. He finally pointed a wing toward it.

"You goofy Indian," he scolded. "Your belly button isn't missing. It's right where you left it."

Then he began poking the tip of his wing at the Indian's belly.

"Just look down," he suggested. "Look down and see."

Freddie looked at where the black hole had just been and found his belly button back where it was supposed to be.

"It's magic!" Freddie shouted. "It's Indian magic!"

"It's not magic," Einstein insisted, spotting a smattering of black paint on Lily's white tail. "It's more like malarkey."

When Freddie saw Einstein looking at Lily's tail, he, too, saw the dab of paint and realized he had been tricked. Then he shouted at the squirrel and the little pink dragon.

"Why, I'll get you two for this," he threatened. "I will think of something extremely wicked to pay you back for this."

Freddie was not happy at all with the two pranksters, for they embarrassed him by painting his belly button as he slept and then told him he'd lost it. As a final insult, they tricked him into putting sewing buttons over his belly button hole, and he had stupidly tried them all. How many of the forest creatures, he wondered, had watched him do that? He felt silly.

"I think I shall leave now," Einstein said, stretching his great wings out and away from his body. "For there is too much tomfoolery going on here on this grand morning."

With that he grunted gruffly and flew off.

Freddie began chasing Lily and Mozart around the trunk of a big tree, but the two pranksters ran off into the woods, leaving Freddie standing in the midst of a pile of sewing buttons. But late that night, as Lily lay in bed, she thought of what the Indian had said about getting even. She knew Freddie the Indian always kept his promises. Sooner or later, she realized, the Indian would find a way to settle the score with Mozart and her.

But that would be another story.

CHAPTER 13

LILY AND THE DRAGON OF LYON

Now just about every day, Lily would take a walk through the Great Green Forest. One bright fall day, Lily decided to take an early morning stroll long before any of the forest animals had risen from their night's sleep. As Lily moved along the path, she felt the early morning dew wetting her fur and the wet grass tickling her feet. As she rounded a bend in the path, Lily spied a glowing light coming from behind a bush, and she crept closer to see from where the light was coming. Just as she suspected, the Forest Wizard was behind the bush, his purple satin robe with flecks of gold in the fabric shimmering in the early morning light. She remembered when she first met the Forest Wizard and how he'd explained to her about her butternut and what might be inside of it. She oftentimes wondered just how much more stuff had accumulated in her butternut since then. Lily saw the wizard was working on something that looked like a tall green box. The door on the box was wide open, and Lily saw dozens of blinking lights flashing inside of the box, with all the colors of the rainbow and even some colors never ever to be found in a rainbow.

Lily continued to hide, not knowing what exactly the Forest Wizard would do to her if he found her spying on him. The wizard held some strange-looking tools in his hands, and it appeared to Lily he was trying to do something with his big green box. Lily was a bit perplexed by the wizard's choice of color for the box. After all, didn't the Great Green Forest already have enough green in it? Why more green? Lily watched the wizard for a while and all of the sudden saw him shake his head while looking at a small tool in his hand. Lily figured the wizard must not have the right tool for whatever he was planning on doing, and she was right, for off went the wizard to find the right tool. Now Lily, being the curious squirrel she was, watched the Forest Wizard depart and emerged from behind the bush. She cautiously walked toward the tall green box, hypnotized by all the lights dancing within it. Her little tail twitched as she looked around the clearing to see if anyone was watching her. Lily, curious as she was, could not resist the temptation of the lights beckoning to her as if she had been hypnotized. In a flash she crept inside the green box. Lily looked around the box and quickly discovered it had no windows. But it did have several brass levers rising from the floor and something fastened to the wall looking like the screen of a drive-in movie theater. Below the screen, a fat red button had been fastened to the wall. Lily was somewhat disappointed because, ever the optimist, she thought there might be something to eat inside, and if she were lucky, it would be chocolate peanut clusters, her favorite food. Then she realized it was time for her to go, for she didn't want the Forest Wizard to return to find out she had been snooping around in his tall green box. It could be a secret project that might one day save the universe, and Lily surely didn't want to mess that up. After all, the wizard might only get one shot at that.

What Lily didn't know was that Poof-Poof the Wind Snipe was blowing around the trees just above her. Now Poof-Poof was, what you might say, that small piece of the wind that liked to play pranks on unsuspecting victims, and Poof-Poof now saw his chance with Lily. You see, Poof-Poof correctly suspected Lily wasn't supposed to be in the Forest Wizard's tall green box in the first place. He spotted Lily just as she was about to exit the box while the Forest Wizard walked back down the path with the tool he'd sought. Poof-Poof circled the tall green box and blew hard on the open door. Inside the box, Lily heard the wind start to blow. As the door began to close, Lily grew alarmed.

SLAM!

The door closed hard with the help of the wind, trapping Lily inside the box. Lily was so frightened by the loud slamming she fell backward, her paw accidentally pushing one of the big brass levers forward. As she tried to balance herself, she accidentally pushed on the fat red button just below the screen.

"Who's in there!" a voice from outside demanded.

"It's me, Lily," Lily answered in a frightened voice. "Who are you?"

"I am the Forest Wizard!" the voice answered. "And you know who I am. I can tell who you are by your voice! Now get out of my time machine, Lily the Squirrel!"

Lily felt a jolt inside the box as the time machine began to move.

"Time machine!" Lily cried. "I thought it might be a secret project to save the universe!"

"Good luck with that, squirrel," the Forest Wizard replied. "I'd have to make a much bigger box to save something that big." He watched the green box move. "Lily, what in the world have you done in there?"

"Nothing," Lily answered. "I just lost my balance. I'm okay now."

Lily felt the box jolting once more.

"Don't touch anything in there," the Forest Wizard warned. "I haven't finished fine-tuning my invention. Don't fool with any of those levers. Don't fool with anything."

"I am afraid I already have," Lily confessed. "Please get me out of here, Forest Wizard."

High above the trees, Poof-Poof the Wind Snipe was laughing uncontrollably, satisfied his prank worked. Suddenly the Forest Wizard shouted.

"Lily, the box is moving! Open the door! Hurry! Get out of there!"

Lily tried in vain to open the door and get out, but the box began spinning and the door would not budge.

"Hang on, Lily!" the Forest Wizard shouted through the door. "Hang on tight!"

Lily felt the box spin and spin, and then the air inside of the box filled with a light blue haze swirling around her. Lily felt her body grow weightless and knew she was moving. She felt a calmness come over her as if she was about to sleep. For a few moments, she was alone, her head foggy, whirling in the sky above the Great Green Forest. Then, as the Forest Wizard and Poof-Poof the Wind Snipe watched, the tall green box disappeared into thin air. Poof-Poof wasn't laughing anymore.

"Oh, woe is me!" the Forest Wizard lamented. "What have I done? What has silly Lily done? Woe is me!"

"Oh, woe is me!" Lily said as the box continued to spin and her head cleared of the fog. Then she spoke to the box. "Whoa, box! Whoa!"

Lily felt the box begin to drop, and she braced her little paws against a wall. It was fortunate Lily braced herself, for the box banged down on something hard and stopped moving. The door opened as if by magic, and Lily found herself on the side of a hill. Around her were lots of trees, like in the Great Green Forest, and Lily figured she must be home. She would find the Forest Wizard, and she would throw herself on his mercy and ask forgiveness, not realizing it was Poof-Poof the Wind Snipe, and not her, who created her predicament. She gazed across the valley and saw rows of plants as far as she could see up and down the valley. On the plants were bundles of fruit. There were huge fields of these things. Lily knew these were grapes, and although there were grapes in the Great Green Forest, there were no vast fields of them like she was seeing. Where exactly was she? Did the Forest Wizard really build a time machine? And if he did, had she traveled through time to a place foreign to her?

As Lily stepped out of the tall green box, she glanced at the screen and read "France, 1172." *What did that mean,* she wondered. Perhaps it's just some kind of clock, and it's merely telling her it's close to lunchtime. She was a bit hungry. Or perhaps it was a sign telling how many people lived here. But, if she was somehow in France, how could there be only 1172 people living in the whole country? How in the world could those few people plant and pick all these grapes covering the hills and valleys as far as she could see?

But then Lily looked at the box and remembered the Forest Wizard had told her his invention was a time machine. Could she possibly be somewhere in France in the year 1172? Lily found that hard to believe but grew excited to think the Forest Wizard's time machine might have taken her back in time. What an adventure this would be! She longed to tell the Forest Wizard his invention worked but was perplexed she couldn't do it right at this moment. The Forest Wizard was quite a few centuries ahead of her right now, and she would have to wait until she got back to speak to him. She shuddered—that is, of course, if she ever managed to get back to the Great Green Forest.

Lily began to walk down the valley. She traveled for about half an hour until she came across a man wearing strange clothes, toiling away in a field, sweating profusely under the midday sun. Lily saw the man's clothes were soiled and tattered, and his shoes were worn so badly Lily could see the man's big toe sticking out of a hole in his left shoe. His shirt looked as if someone had cut and sewn a burlap potato sack into a baggy shirt, and the stiff pants he wore seemed to be made of hair, as if his tailor merely draped a deer hide over his legs and then just walked away. His shoes seemed to grow up his ankles and were made of something soft. And the soft cloth sagged and wrinkled. He struggled with a hoe, chopping at the soil with the tool.

"Who are you?" Lily asked the man.

"I'm a serf," the man replied, studying Lily. "And I usually don't talk to squirrels, especially white ones. In fact, you're the first white squirrel I've ever seen in my entire life."

"Well, that's okay," Lily shot back. "I'm Lily. And, by the way, where do you surf around here?"

"Why, I serf right here," the man answered, raising his hoe. "Where do you think a serf would serf?"

Lily looked around her and saw only fields. There was no water anywhere. Lily had yet to understand in France at this time a serf was simply a shabbily dressed servant who worked like a dog for a rich landowner and for very little reward. Surf was the fun stuff people did on waves, and that word was invented hundreds of years later by people who wore wild and colorful surf stuff. There lay the confusion as she continued to speak to the man.

"Your surfboard?" she asked. "Where is the surfboard?"

The man looked at Lily rather quizzically.

"Lily, my little squirrel friend," he answered, "a serf is never bored, but I sure would like to be once in a while. Only the well-off can afford to be bored. We always have more work to do than time to do it, and when we're not working, we are always running away from the Danged and Dreaded creature known as the Dragon of Lyon."

Lily didn't quite understand how the conversation switched so abruptly from surfing to dragons, but that never stopped her from having an adventure before and it wouldn't now.

"The Dragon of Lyon?" she asked. "What's that?"

The man pointed to a castle in the distance.

"That is Lyon," he explained. "And we are terrorized by a dragon who lives right down the road from the castle. He is always chasing us and stealing our food when we try to take it to market. You must be new around here, squirrel, or you'd cringe in terror at the very mention of the name Dragon of Lyon."

"Well, I have never seen a dragon that big," Lily answered. "And yes, my friend who surfs with no board, I am quite new around here. But I have a friend named Mozart who is a little pink dragon even smaller than me and plays music on his magical mushrooms. Mozart wouldn't hurt a flea."

Lily almost corrected her words right then for she once watched as Mozart slapped a flea off his stomach during a drum concert and sent the poor insect bouncing off one of the mushroom drums and into a pile of leaves. But she thought better of it.

"Your Mozart sounds like a real sissy of a dragon," the man smirked. "Pint-sized lizard is more like it with a sissy pink color and a sissy music maker. And what kind of a name is Mozart? Sounds like someone mixed up some letters and never got them straightened out."

"Mozart was actually a great–" Lily began, checking her words. How could she tell someone who didn't know what a surfboard was that Mozart was a great composer who wasn't going to be born for hundreds of years yet and that his music would change the world? And the name Mozart would be forever revered and loved by all. She'd just better keep all those facts to herself, she decided.

"Well," she explained to the man. "Mozart is what he is. But per-haps I will go to Lyon and catch a glimpse of your Danged and Dreaded

Dragon of Lyon for myself. By the way, this Dragon of Lyon doesn't happen to shoot fire from his mouth, does he?"

"Oh, yes," the man boasted proudly. "Gigantic flames ten feet long. Why, the beast can roast a cow in two minutes flat. Bet your little Mozart can't do that."

"Not really," Lily answered. "He can only poof out little pink smoke most of the time. Unless you tick him off, his flame is pretty useless."

"A dragon without a flame," the man scoffed. "Better tell him to remain in his prissy little world, squirrel. He wouldn't survive long in this one."

Lily couldn't help but think about how true the man's words were. She turned and started up the path to Lyon and then spoke once more.

"Maybe we can go surfing together sometime," she said.

The man looked up from his work and rolled his eyes.

"I don't like serfing," the man said. "Like I already told you, I only serf because I have to. I wouldn't want my family to go hungry, you know."

What a strange little man, Lily thought as she turned toward Lyon. Nobody has to surf if they don't want to. One could always choose to fish instead or just wade near the shore if they wanted to be in the water. His logic was completely confusing to her.

It took Lily several hours to walk to the castle at Lyon because the trail upon which she walked was rocky and winding. It was nearly sunset and crowds of people were coming inside for the night. Nobody wanted to be caught outside the sturdy castle walls after dark with the Danged and Dreaded Dragon of Lyon. Lily watched as the castle guards raised the drawbridge, closing the castle until dawn and denying the dragon access inside.

Lily decided to go exploring inside the castle for it was her first time ever being in one. She soon came across a group of knights sitting at an enormous round table, eating a great feast. At the head of the table sat the King of the Castle, speaking to his brave knights. Lily saw the grand meal on the table and realized how hungry she was from traveling all day. Her last meal had been thousands of miles away and hundreds of years ahead of where she was now. She was ravenous and her stomach began making gurgling noises. She spied a knight's helmet on the wall and put it on her head. Although she realized the helmet was a tad big for her head, she knew now she could approach the table to get the same food the knights were eating. She planned to fill her plate and get out of there before anyone discovered she was a squirrel. As she began to fill her plate with grapes and nuts, the king spoke.

"I ask you again, who among my brave knights will go forth tomorrow and do battle with the Danged and Dreaded Dragon of Lyon?" the King demanded, pounding his fist on the table.

Lily figured she'd better hurry things up a bit, for she wanted no part of any Danged and Dreaded Dragon. That's all she'd need, to get roasted in dragon flames in France hundreds of years before she was even born. She wondered how she'd explain it to her friends in the Great Green Forest. She could just visualize how the conversation would go.

"So, Lily," Robert the Moose would ask, "how and where did you get that nasty burn on your rear end?"

She knew she would be forced to answer, "Well, I got caught in the flames of the Danged and Dreaded Dragon of Lyon six thousand miles from here and about eight hundred years ago." Yes, that would go over well. Her friends would most likely grab her and put her in one of those straitjackets she'd heard about. At least she'd finally understand why they were used.

Lily spotted a peppershaker on the table and began to shake pepper onto a lovely bunch of grapes and nuts she'd put on her plate. A rather portly knight next to Lily waved his napkin as he placed it in his lap, and the breeze he created blew pepper through the holes in Lily's helmet as the king spoke once more.

"I ask you once more, brave knights," he pleaded, "who among you will go forth tomorrow and do battle with the Danged and Dreaded Dragon of Lyon?"

Lily's nose began to twitch as the pepper found its way up her nostrils. Suddenly, the great room was filled with tremendous sneeze that echoed through the room and down the hallways of the castle.

"Ah-ah-ah-ah-choo-oo-oo-ooh!"

Lily sneezed so hard the force of the sneeze launched her little body into the air. She somersaulted as she reached her high point but managed to land with her feet on the table. Her helmet came down over her face as grapes and nuts rained down around her. To her amazement, she found the king smiling at her as she spied at him through the eye slit of the helmet.

"Ah, my gallant knight," the king said with a satisfied smile. "You must surely be the bravest knight in all of my realm. You are certainly not my biggest knight—that I can see clearly, for your entire body fits quite nicely inside your helmet. But on this splendid evening, your heart certainly is the biggest one in my kingdom. For of the many brave knights around this table, only you, Little Knight, volunteered to help your king when much bigger knights failed to do so. Tomorrow you will venture forth as my champion to do battle with the Danged and Dreaded Dragon of Lyon."

Lily had no idea how she'd managed to get herself in this fix, or what to do next, so she addressed the king.

"Oh, Great King, I will surely do battle with your dragon. But just to refresh my memory a little bit, tell me, just how big is this Danged and Dreaded Dragon of Lyon?"

You see, Lily was thinking about Mozart the Dragon, her little pink friend back at the Great Green Forest. She was kind of hoping the Dragon of Lyon was just about Mozart's size, regardless of what the serf told her earlier.

"Why, everyone around here knows how big the Dragon of Lyon is," the king answered. "He is twenty-three feet long and eleven feet high, give or take a few inches. Just your average-sized dragon, you see. A knight of your character, small though you may be, should have no problem with that rascal at all. Just be thankful you're not a squirrel or a rabbit. Rumor is he loves to flame-broil those little guys and eat them for breakfast."

Lily gulped and her little legs began to quiver as she tried to imagine something eleven feet tall standing before her, particularly since the beast apparently had a flare for flame-broiled squirrels. The king raised his glass and all the knights around the table did likewise.

"A toast," he said, "To... sorry, what did you say your name was again, Little Knight?"

"Lily," Lily said through the slit in her helmet. "It's Lily."

"To Sir Lily," the king said, hoisting his glass and gulping. Then he added, "I don't believe I've ever known a knight named Lily before. That might take some getting used to. But times seem to be changing and we must change with them."

The next morning, with all his subjects assembled, the king ordered the drawbridge lowered and watched from his perch on the castle wall as Lily, engulfed in her enormous helmet, began walking down the long road leading to the dragon's cave. It didn't take Lily long to discard the clumsy steel helmet and heavy sword the king had given her, for each object alone weighed more than she did. As Lily walked along, she came to a bend in the road. She halted. Bends in roads always seemed to indicate something was about to happen, and not necessarily something good. Lily peeked around the bend but saw nothing threatening, only a large green hill a stone's throw away. Lily rounded the bend and drew close to the hill. The hill rose up right in the middle of the road, and Lily thought it was odd for a hill to do so. A hill was a hill and didn't need to be in the middle of a road where people would have to walk around it. Suddenly Lily's body shook and her tail bristled. The hill quivered. Her little whiskers twitched. This was not a hill at all! This was the Danged and Dreaded Dragon of Lyon in the middle of the road! The dragon was sleeping, and tiny clouds of smoke escaped from its nose every time he let loose a snore.

Now Lily had her own plan, one she thought up during the long night in the castle. It was a clever plan where she could avoid any sort of encounter with anything that might want to eat her while allowing her to make her escape back to the Forest Wizard's time machine. Lily figured she would sneak past the dragon and continue down the road, and no one would be the wiser until she was far away and back in the time machine. However, from behind her came a roaring sound of cheers from the crowd watching from the castle walls. The loud cheers traveled through the morning air and woke the Danged and Dreaded Dragon of Lyon. Lily watched his body quiver in the cool morning air.

The dragon's big fiery green eyes opened, and his mammoth head lifted from the ground, towering in front of her. The dragon's eyes were the shape of large pecans, but green, with a long black line running across the middle of the green. Its nose was long but blunt at the end, as if the beast had run smack into a door and flattened it. The end of the nose curled slightly upward. Lily's little body shook as the dragon spewed putrid-smelling breath on her from above. She couldn't help thinking it was a little early in the morning for a steam bath.

"Well, what have we here?" the dragon scoffed. "You are just in time to be my breakfast." He nodded toward the castle. "I suppose they told you I absolutely love squirrel meat, not as tender as the meat of a starving serf, and not as much, but you'll do, squirrel." He stared at Lily. "Hmm… a white squirrel to boot. Fancy that. I've never eaten one of those before." He licked his lips. "I can't wait to flame-broil you, squirrel."

Lily knew she had to think of something quickly.

"You know," she cautioned, "you are wrong about that, Dragon. Squirrel meat is actually pretty bad for your health." She put her paws around her belly and puffed up, pretending to be fat. "See here, all this fat I carry around would clog up those clean arteries of yours if you eat it. In fact, I happen to know of one dragon that ate so much squirrel fat he clogged up his flamethrower and couldn't hurl fire for a month. Everyone laughed at him and threw marshmallows at his head. It was quite sad to see such a majestic beast humbled in such a way."

"I don't believe you," the dragon snorted. "There's no such thing as a marshmallow."

The dragon was right. Marshmallows hadn't been invented yet. They were hundreds of years into the future. It's no wonder the dragon didn't believe her story. Lily looked up at the dragon's great head and decided it was time to bring out her good luck piece. Curled up in the squirrel's right ear, hidden quite nicely, was a large pink flamingo feather. Lily pulled it out and hid it behind her back. As she did, the feather uncurled and straightened up like a sword in her paw. It ran up her back and Lily felt it tickling her neck. The gentle tickling gave the squirrel a brilliant idea. The dragon lowered its huge head, sniffing at Lily's fur. Huge drops of saliva rolled over his lower lip and plopped to the ground as he smelled the delectable scent of the squirrel.

"Oh, yummy," he said. "Yummy–yummy–yummy. Looks like I get to have roasted squirrel for breakfast. I must admit once more that I've never eaten the meat of a white squirrel." He drooled. "I'm really looking forward to this."

Lily gripped the feather tighter in her paw and thought hard about the idea forming in her mind. She remembered how, during the previous morning, the wet grass tickled her feet as she walked in the Great Green Forest.

"Okay then, you big overgrown smelly lizard!" she shouted, mustering all the fake courage she could muster. "Go ahead and eat me! See if I care. But I'm not going to show you the neat thing I have in my paw. If you burn me, you'll burn it. But then you'll never know what you missed out on."

A funny look came over the dragon's face. For you see, dragons are naturally curious, and even more so when they might miss out on something secret. It just didn't seem right to the dragon that he should eat this little squirrel without first finding out what was hidden behind her back.

"Well, what's in your paw?" he snorted as smoke blew from his snout. "Show me, I say!"

"Why should I show you, you big green toad?" Lily answered and then added sarcastically, "What are you going to do if I don't show you—eat me? That's going to happen anyway so there's nothing in it for me if I do show you."

Now the dragon was kind of in a fix and he knew it. He was also aware no one was to blame for his predicament but his own bullying self. He knew the crafty squirrel wasn't going to show him what was in her paw without some sort of reward. The only reward he could give the squirrel was her freedom, and he didn't want to do that, for he wanted his breakfast. But he thought he would tell her a little fib and get her to show him what lay hidden behind her.

"Okay, little squirrel," he said. "I'll tell you what I'll do. If you show me what is in your paw, I will let you go."

"The name is Lily," Lily said. "And, according to the king back there in Lyon, it's Sir Lily."

"Do tell," the dragon scoffed. "A girl knight. Now I know you're telling tales. No self-respecting king would send a girl knight out to slay a dragon, especially a girl knight who also happens to be a squirrel, and a prissy little white one at that."

Lily wished she could take the dragon back with her in the Forest Wizard's time machine. She would show him girl squirrels had come a long way and could now do lots of things only boy squirrels used to do. Although the dragon's eyes were quite big and green, what he would learn there would really open them up to how things had progressed.

"Nevertheless," Lily answered. "It is what it is and that is all that it is." She jiggled her arm up and down behind her back. "Now, do you promise you'll let me go if I show you this green marble in my paw?"

"Ah-ha!" the dragon shot back, "You have a green marble in your paw! You have made a big mistake, Lily, my scrumptious morning breakfast. You should have been smarter than to have matched wits with a dragon."

"Oh, did I say marble?" Lily laughed. "That's what was in my paw yesterday. Today I have something else. Sorry about that. I hope my little verbal misquote doesn't affect our agreement."

The dragon scowled.

"I ought to eat you right now for fooling me like that," he threatened.

"Okay, go ahead then," Lily answered, closing her eyes while holding out a paw. "Cook me and up in smoke with me goes this nifty prize behind my back."

"Oooh," the dragon moaned, quite perplexed by the turn of events. "Okay, then. I give up. I swear by all that is holy I will not eat you." He leaned over, trying to peer behind the squirrel's back but could not. "Now let's just get this over with. Let me see what's behind your back."

"Okay," Lily said. "Come closer and I will show you what is in my paw."

The dragon leaned toward Lily.

"Closer," Lily said.

The dragon leaned down further.

"Just a little closer," Lily said. "I want you to get a good look."

Lily could see the dragon's mouth open right above her as he lowered his head toward the ground. The dragon now bent so low Lily could touch him. Lily quickly stepped below the dragon's neck and held the flamingo feather against his skin. Then she began tickling his neck with the feather, moving the very tip of the fluffy feather back and forth along his scaly green skin.

"Gitchy-gitchy-goo," she said as she swished the feather rapidly across the dragon's neck. "Gitchy-gitchy-goo."

At first the dragon didn't know what to do about this strange ritual happening below him. The squirrel disappeared from his view, but as he felt the feather moving against his neck, he began to giggle.

"Ha-ha-ha-ha!" he roared. "Ha-ha-ha-ha!"

As the dragon laughed, Lily began making longer strokes across his neck, rubbing the flamingo feather up and down in longer and longer strokes. This made the dragon laugh even harder, so hard smoke escaped from his nostrils in puffs of happiness.

"Ha-ha-ha-ha!" the dragon roared again. "Ha-ha-ha-ha!"

Lily kept tickling the dragon all morning and well into the afternoon. Just about when she thought her arm would fall off from exhaustion, the dragon collapsed. His huge body flopped to the ground, creating a small depression as it did so. The Danged and Dreaded Dragon of Lyon was spent, and he knew it.

"Stop, Lily!" he pleaded. "Ha-ha-ha-ha! Please stop, and I won't eat you, I promise. Just stop! I can't take any more of this!"

Lily tickled him even harder.

"Ha-ha-ha-ha!" he laughed. "Please stop! I'm begging you! I'll do anything if you'll just stop tickling me! I'm about to wet myself."

"I will only stop," Lily answered, "if you promise to stop being such a bully to the people of Lyon. I must have your dragon promise on it. You must find something to munch on other than humans and squirrels."

"Ha-ha-ha-ha!" replied the dragon, rolling in the dirt from laughing so hard. Hundreds of green scales littered the ground around him after they fell from his body as he rolled around. "Okay, I will give you my dragon promise. Just touch the inside of my belly button with your paw."

The Danged and Dreaded Dragon of Lyon turned his belly button to Lily and she pressed her paw deep inside of it. When she saw yellow sparks flying from the belly button, she knew the deal had been sealed. Lily stopped tickling the dragon's neck. The dragon lay in the road for a few minutes, exhausted by all his laughing.

"Now," Lily commanded, "we will go see the king, and tell him you will be a nice dragon from now on and won't eat any more of his subjects or he won't have anyone left to pick all those grapes around the castle."

"Okay, Lily," the dragon answered meekly. "A dragon promise is a promise that must be kept. After all, a paw in a belly button is a paw that has performed magic. No dragon would ever break his word after that, no matter how dirty and despicable they otherwise might be."

"Well," Lily answered happily. "It's nice to know decency and despicability can sometimes sit side by side in the same room."

Lily sat upon the dragon's head as the great beast began walking toward the castle, the sun setting behind them. Inside the castle, the sun played tricks on the guards who protected the road to the castle, and as they saw the dragon walking toward them, they thought the huge beast was about to attack Lyon. Torches were lit at all the battlements, and all the archers prepared for a do-or-die, winner-take-all battle with the Danged and Dreaded Dragon of Lyon. All thoughts of the Little Knight Lily sent out that morning to slay the dragon had long been forgotten.

As Lily and the dragon approached the castle, they saw the torches lighting the archers in the windows.

"Stop!" Lily shouted, "Do not shoot the Dragon of Lyon!"

"Is that you, Sir Lily?" the king shouted down from high in one of the towers. "Are you deaf, Little Knight? I said slay him, not play with him! What are you doing sitting on top of the Danged and Dreaded Dragon of Lyon?"

"Yes, Great King!" Lily shouted back. "It is I. I have great news for you. You can cut out that part about Danged and Dreaded. From now on he'll just be the Dragon of Lyon. He will be a loyal and trustworthy friend to your kingdom and all its people."

Lily jumped off the dragon and entered the castle. For the remainder of the night, as the dragon slept outside the castle walls, Lily told the king and all his knights how the dragon promised not to bully or bite, or even drool, for that matter, on any person of Lyon.

By virtue of his position as king, and because there hadn't been many opportunities lately to award medals in Lyon, the king bestowed upon Lily the Royal Order of the Bulbs Medallion. It was actually a medal normally given to people who were quite good at growing flowers. But in this case, that requirement was unanimously waived, and the medal was awarded to the Little Knight named Lily. After all, what's in a medal but metal—it's the thought that really counts.

The king, quite pleased with the dragon sleeping peacefully outside his castle, now proclaimed a new title for the giant beast. Instead of the Danged and Dreaded Dragon of Lyon, the dragon's new title would become the Dapper and Delightful Dragon of Lyon, and all subjects of his realm would address the dragon in that manner. Lily assured the king that from now on, the Dapper and Delightful Dragon of Lyon would feast only on grapes, dandelions, buttercups, or assorted nuts and berries, either roasted or raw, depending on the depth of his hunger or the season of the year.

Early the next morning, the now Dapper and Delightful Dragon of Lyon awoke to thuds on his body as something bounced up and down on his skin. As he opened his eyes, the dragon could only smile as he watched the children of Lyon playing on his huge body. As they jumped, green scales bounced up and down among them, and the young ones giggled with joy. From then on the dragon was often seen in the fields next to the castle, watching over the children as the serfs worked neaby.

As for Lily, she managed to sneak from the castle the next day with her Royal Order of the Bulbs Medallion and found the Forest Wizard's time machine. Lily, being a rather bright squirrel, figured out how to get the machine to work, which didn't take much—just pushing the lever the opposite direction from how she pulled it to travel back in time to Lyon and then giving the red button a firm push. The tall green box transported Lily in the blink of an eye back to the Great Green Forest to the exact spot where she departed from in the first place. As she opened the door, she found an infuriated Forest Wizard waiting for her, his foot tapping angrily and a rage in his eyes. However, Lily had thought about what she would do upon her arrival. She placed the Royal Order of the Bulbs Medallion over the Forest Wizard's head, telling him it was made from special metals and formed in the fires of a dragon's mouth. The Forest Wizard, always one to appreciate the art of magic, gratefully accepted his prize.

It was a gift, Lily told him, from the Dapper and Delightful Dragon of Lyon.

CHAPTER 14

LILY MEETS AN ELECAN'T

Early one morning Lily woke up from a terrible night's sleep. She arose groggy, and it took her a few minutes to understand why her sleep had been so disturbed. Quite a racket began sometime after midnight and continued until dawn broke. Then she realized what had happened, for the same event repeated itself every year at just about this time. The circus was passing through the countryside and camped, as it normally did, in a large meadow just outside the boundaries of the Great Green Forest. Lily realized the circus noise kept her from getting her normal beauty sleep. Lily leaped from her bed and realized she was still very tired. A quick plunge into the chilly waters of Paula's Pond might be just the thing she needed to start her day and wake her up. The squirrel grabbed her bath towel, climbed down the Big Oak, and began to wander in the direction of the pond. She walked, whistling a little tune to cheer her up. As she moved along the path, the sun crept over the horizon and began to shine into the forest. Lily continued on until, in the shadows, she tripped over a rather large log that had fallen next to the path. The log stuck out just enough to catch her leg.

"Ouch!" the log shouted. "Watch where you're going, you clumsy fool!"

Now this upset poor Lily because she was not accustomed to logs screaming in pain in the Great Green Forest, or saying anything at all for that matter. Lily, frightened by the abrupt shouting, ran down the path a little way and then stopped to look back. To her amazement, the talking log had vanished. As you well know by now, Lily is a rather curious squirrel, and something within her made her circle back to search for the strange log that had called her a fool, for she never in all her travels encountered a talking piece of wood, although she did have a yearning to one day meet Pinocchio. It was a fact that in the Great Green Forest, there were hundreds of logs that had fallen over the years. She walked to the spot where she had tripped, her tail twitching nervously as she searched the area around her. Just as Lily began to think she imagined the whole incident, she saw something stir in the long grass in front of her.

"Who's in there?" Lily demanded. "Come out of there!"

At first there was silence in the grass, but then a soft voice spoke.

"There's no one in here," the voice said meekly.

"No one in there?" Lily asked. "Then who's speaking?" Then she added, "A voice needs someone behind it or it won't work. Any fool would know that."

"How do you know anyone is speaking?" the voice asked. "After all, I might only be the wind sweeping through the branches of a tree. I might be a wind snipe."

"I know the voice of Poof-Poof the Wind Snipe," Lily answered. "And you're not him. He can never finish a whole sentence without taking a breath, the old windbag. Besides, if he were in there, the grass would be moving as he spoke."

"Well, little squirrel," the voice replied. "It is of no concern to you who I am. Why don't you just take your towel and go get your bath."

"My name is Lily," Lily answered. "And I'm not taking a bath. That dumb circus made so much noise last night I couldn't get any sleep. I'm going to jump in the cool pond water to help me wake up, as if it's any concern to you."

"Hey, we didn't make that much noise," the voice answered. "We actually were quite–oops–"

136

"Ah-ha!" Lily pounced, walking into the grass and peeking over to see who owned the voice. To her astonishment, Lily found a small elephant hiding in the grass. "You're with the circus!"

"Well I guess I am," the little elephant replied.

"And you're an elephant!" Lily exclaimed. "An honest-to-goodness real live elephant right here in the Great Green Forest."

"Shhh!" the animal warned, placing the end of his trunk over his mouth. "Be quiet! I have run away from the circus, and I don't want anyone to know where I am."

"You ran away from the circus?" Lily asked. "I thought elephants loved the circus."

"They do," he replied. Then he lowered his head in shame. "You see I'm not an elephant at all. My name is Eli and I'm an Elecan't."

"An Elecan't?" Lily asked. "What in the world is an Elecan't? I've never heard of such an animal. Just how are you any different from any other elephant? I don't understand."

"That's just what they tell me," the Elecan't replied, holding up his trunk and waving it toward Lily. "As you can plainly see, I have a very tiny trunk. It's not my fault though. I was born with it."

Lily looked at the Elecan't trunk, and thought, *perhaps it is kind of a short trunk*. But not being an expert in such matters, she wasn't sure.

"Well, Eli," Lily said. "You are not very old at all. Perhaps your tiny trunk will get much longer as you grow. You know how some parts of the body grow slower than others. Maybe that's all it is."

"No, it won't," Eli said sadly. "They said I am doomed to always have a tiny trunk."

"Who?" asked Lily. "Who told you that?"

"Why, all the other elephants at the circus," Eli explained. "They told me I was an Elecan't. It's because I am an elephant who can't."

"Can't?" Lily asked. "Can't what?"

"Can't," Eli replied. "Can't do anything. Anything an elephant is supposed to do."

"I don't believe you can't do anything." Lily said, "For I can tell by looking at you that you are very strong."

Hearing what Lily said about him, the Elecan't perked up a bit. He held his head just a little higher.

"I used to think that myself," he said. "But that was before I found I couldn't do the normal elephant stuff."

"Elephant stuff?" Lily asked. "What is elephant stuff?"

"You know," Eli said, "stuff like moving big logs and boulders and helping put up the Big Top at the circus. My trunk is so tiny I can't wrap it around those big tent posts. The other elephants tell me I'm just in the way and to sit down and just watch them work. Then, of course, there is the trumpeting part. Trumpeting is the most important thing an elephant can do. All my elephant friends raise their big trunks and fill the air with an enormous trumpeting sound while shooting out magnificent gobs of gray-green gobbledygook. But the best I can do is just blow a little toot with no gook. When they hear my toot, every other elephant laughs at me."

"Well," Lily asked, "what are you going to do now, Eli the Elecan't? I mean you just can't hide in the grass forever. You will get hungry in a while, and besides, autumn is coming, and you will look pretty silly just standing there alone when the grass withers and falls to the ground. Everyone will think you're a boulder."

The Elecan't looked around at the little patch of grass, imagining how silly it would be to stand there after the grass was gone.

"You are right, Lily," he said. "But what am I to do?"

Lily thought for a moment about what the Elecan't said. A brilliant idea came to her.

"I know! I know!" she said. "We can go ask Einstein."

"Einstein?" the Elecan't asked. "What is an Einstein?"

"Why, Einstein is an owl," Lily replied. "And he's a very wise owl. He will be able to help you."

"Okay, Lily," the Elecan't replied. "I'm willing to try anything that might get me back to the circus. Let's go see this owl you speak of so highly."

Lily and the Elecan't ventured down one of the paths of the Great Green Forest until they came to the tree where Einstein the Wise Old Owl made his home. Lily saw by looking into the hole in the trunk that

Einstein was still sleeping. He even wore dark blinders over his eyes to keep out the light. The owl was a late sleeper, and everyone in the Great Green Forest knew it. Lily picked up a large walnut and tossed it at the hole in the tree. The walnut flew through the hole and hit the poor owl right on his forehead, making a hollow thunking sound as it did so.

"Very irregular, very irregular," the owl said, waking up and looking around to find nothing but darkness. "Who dares wake me up at this hour of the day? I should give you a good pecking on the top of your head!"

"It's me, Einstein!" Lily shouted from the ground. "It's Lily the Squirrel."

"Very irregular," the owl repeated, "to be awakened from my sleep! And so terribly abruptly too! Why, this is quite uncivilized! You should know better, Lily!"

Einstein pulled off his blinders with a flip of one wing and looked down at the squirrel standing on the floor of the forest.

"I'm sorry, Einstein," Lily said. "But I am afraid I have a rather pressing issue that only you, the wisest animal in the forest, can resolve."

The owl's chest feathers puffed up with pride at hearing what the squirrel said about him.

"Of course, of course," Einstein said. "By all means, my good friend, I can help you. But say, what is that possum doing standing next to you? And look at the size of him!"

Lily saw a sad look form on the face of the Elecan't.

"Don't worry, Eli," she assured him, "Einstein meant no harm. You see, he is an owl, and they don't see very well when they first wake up. He's just guessing what you are. He didn't mean to offend you."

"That's okay," the Elecan't answered. "I am used to being called names. It comes from having a tiny trunk."

Lily shouted up at the owl.

"Einstein, this is my friend Eli," she explained. "He's not a possum—he's an Elecan't. And he badly needs your help."

"My help?" Einstein asked. "Why, whatever would an... what did you call him—whatever would an Elecan't need with my help?"

Lily pointed to the Elecan't trunk.

"His tiny trunk," she explained. "He was born with a tiny trunk. All the other elephants in the circus are making fun of him because of it. It's not his fault at all, as you can see. Can you do anything to make his tiny trunk a bit longer?"

Einstein thought for a moment and then scratched his head with the tip of his wing.

"I'll tell you what," he said. "Let me sleep a bit more. My brain runs better when I'm asleep and don't have all that annoying awake stuff to worry about. To tell you the truth, my head hurts a bit from that dumb nut you threw at me a minute ago—thank you very much. You two come back tonight after I've had some time to contemplate, and we will solve this tiny trunk problem under the light of the full moon."

Einstein immediately put his blinders back on and closed his eyes to resume his sleep. The owl was soon snoring away as Lily and the Elecan't went off in search of something to eat. That afternoon, as Lily and the Elecan't played by the pond, the Elecan't told Lily all sorts of stories about the circus. The Elecan't told the squirrel the circus was quite fun when no one was teasing him about his short trunk. When evening came, Lily and the Elecan't returned to the tree and looked up at the hole. To their surprise, the owl was still asleep.

"Hey, Einstein!" Lily shouted. "You are supposed to be helping us. Remember?"

The owl turned his head and opened his eyes as he once more pulled off his blinders.

"Oh yes," he said, looking at the Elecan't. "Still the problem with the tiny trunk I take it?"

"Well," Lily asked impatiently, "have you found the solution?"

"Quite correctly, quite correctly," Einstein answered. "I have found the solution. But first you must go find Freddie the Indian and Robert the Moose. Bring them here to the tree. Tell them they must find a very thick and strong piece of rope. And hurry, the full moon is about to rise."

Lily and the Elecan't scurried off to do as the owl instructed. In a short while they returned with Freddie the Indian and Robert the Moose as the full moon lit the forest around them. Dangling from one of Robert's antlers was a very thick and strong-looking piece of rope.

Einstein flew from his perch in the tree and landed on Robert's antler. In his wing the owl held a long piece of wood.

"What is that?" Lily asked.

"Oh, this thing?" Einstein answered, holding up the piece of wood. "Why, this is nothing more than an ordinary ruler."

"What are we going to do with a ruler?" Freddie the Indian asked.

"Very simple," Einstein said, winking at them. "We are going to measure how long the Elecan't tiny trunk is before we stretch it. It will be a good thing to know if I ever decide to write a paper about it—you know, for science."

"Stretch my tiny trunk," the Elecan't said in a worried voice. "Won't that be dangerous? It's the only trunk I have, and I've grown pretty fond of it, tiny as it is. What happens if it gets pulled off? Then what would I do? I'd be worse off than I am now. I'd be little more than a glorified hog if that happened."

"Well, if that happened," Robert said, "maybe you *would* be a possum." The moose looked at the rear end of the Elecan't. "But you'd need a much longer tail."

"That's not funny!" the Elecan't snorted. "I don't intend to spend the rest of my life hanging from a tree branch by my tail."

"He was joking," Lily told the Elecan't. She shot an annoyed look at the moose.

"There is always a risk in doing something," Einstein explained. "But do you want to traipse around for the rest of your life with a tiny trunk? Do you want to be teased forever?"

"Not really," the Elecan't said. "That doesn't sound like it would be fun at all."

"Well then, Elecan't," the owl replied, "then we are going to have to stretch your tiny trunk to get it to come out. Who knows, it might just be knotted up in there—it might be just that simple. We might get you another foot or so by merely unraveling a knot. And I have brought a ruler so we can measure just how much stretch we get as we go."

As he sat on Robert's antler, the owl took the piece of wood and measured the Elecan't trunk from start to finish. He found the tiny trunk was exactly twelve inches long.

"You have a foot," Einstein declared.

"I have four of them," the Elecan't replied. "But don't we know that already?"

"No," Einstein corrected. "I mean your tiny trunk is exactly one foot long."

"Oh," the Elecan't said. "How long should it be?"

Einstein scratched his head with his wing, thinking about the question as the full moon rose over his shoulder.

"I guess," he replied, "the question is not how long it should be, but how long do you want it to be."

The Elecan't pondered the owl's statement for a moment. No one had ever asked him anything quite like that before.

"I want my trunk long enough where I can be called an Elephant instead of an Elecan't," he declared. "All I want is a respectable trunk—a trunk to be proud of—a trunk I can toot about."

"Fair enough," Einstein said, shaking his head with approval. "Knowing that, we can go from there."

Then he turned to Freddie the Indian and Robert the Moose.

"You two, unwind the rope from Robert's antler, and lay it out on the ground. And Lily, you take the Elecan't over to that low tree over there, the one with the fork toward the bottom."

And that's what they did. As Freddie and Robert rolled out the rope, Lily and Einstein placed the head of the Elecan't on the fork of the tree so his chin rested right in the bottom of the fork. The Elecan't was now secured with his tiny trunk sticking out.

"Now, bring one end of that rope to me," Einstein instructed.

Freddie dragged one end of the rope to Einstein, and the owl carefully tied the rope around the very end of the tiny trunk. He then instructed Freddie to give the rope a few sharp tugs to make sure it was fastened securely to the tiny trunk of the Elecan't. Freddie gave the rope a sharp jerk and the trunk stretched out tightly.

"Okay," Einstein instructed. "We are going to pull on the rope and stretch the trunk a bit at a time. Freddie and Robert, you two can pull on the rope, and I will measure how much the tiny trunk is stretching. But we must pull very slowly and very gently. Remember, we just want to stretch the tiny trunk, not pull it off. And we don't want to pull on it too much or the Elecan't will be tripping over his way-too-long trunk, okay?"

That being said, Freddie wrapped the rope twice around Robert's antlers and then grasped the rope in his big hands. Lily hopped on Robert's antlers and directed them.

"Everyone ready?" Einstein asked, placing the ruler flat against the tiny trunk.

"Ready," Lily declared, looking over at Freddie.

"Pull!" Einstein shouted. "Pull, me hearties!" Einstein was well aware 'hearties' was a name normally given to sailors, but since they were kind of sailing through uncharted waters, he figured he could call them that now.

The moon rose higher as Freddie and Robert pulled on the rope. Moonbeams danced off the rope as it strained in the cool night air. The tiny trunk straightened out, and the little Elecan't began to feel the stretch as Freddie and Robert pulled gently. Gradually they could feel they were making progress and took a step backward. Einstein stood on the fork of the tree with the ruler.

"Thirteen inches," Einstein said, smiling enthusiastically as he measured. "It's working. Tug a bit harder."

Freddie and Robert pulled again as Lily shouted encouragement to them. Again, Einstein pressed the ruler against the Elecan't.

"Fifteen inches," he shouted with joy. "We have stretched the trunk three full inches." He looked around, satisfied by what he saw. "By the way, it has been noted in all the books I've read on this subject that any trunk over fifteen inches cannot be considered a tiny trunk. It's right there in bold print, in the Periodical of Pachyderm Publication, page 101, plain as the nose on your face." He turned to the Elecan't. "Or, plain as the trunk on yours." He addressed the group. "We are making splendid progress, friends. Just one more wee tug and I think we'll have it."

What Freddie and Robert did not see in the moonlight was a small stand of wet grass behind them. As they backed up again, they both slipped on the grass, causing them to abruptly jerk backward and land on their rear ends.

"Wow!" declared the owl, "Now that was some pull!" He laid the ruler against the trunk of the Elecan't. "Amazing! We now have a twenty-two-inch trunk! That's ten full inches of stretch! That's some trunk now!"

Einstein looked into the Elecan't eyes.

"Do you want more stretch?" he asked. "Or is this the respectable trunk you have hoped for?"

Einstein held a mirror in front of the Elecan't and showed him his outstretched trunk.

"Why, it's beautiful!" the Elecan't declared. "It's just beautiful! It's a grand work of art. Just grand."

"Okay, then," Einstein commanded happily. "Let's untie the rope."

The Elecan't jumped up and down excitedly as Freddie untied the rope from his trunk. "I can't wait to use my big trunk," he said happily. "No more cracks from the other elephants about a tiny trunk. No siree!"

The Elecan't walked over to a huge rock and picked it up easily. He tossed it into the air and caught it with his longer trunk. Then he flung it as far as he could.

"Look at me!" he giggled. "Look at what I can do!"

He walked over to a tree measuring about four inches in diameter and wrapped his longer trunk around it. As Freddie, Robert, Lily, and Einstein watched with amazement, the Elecan't pulled the tree from the ground and swung it around his head. When he was finished, he set the tree back into its hole and stamped the dirt around it back into place.

"Whoopee!" the Elecan't shouted, dancing around in the light of the moon. "Look at me! Look at me and my terrific trunk!"

The Elecan't had never been this happy in his whole life.

"What are you going to do now, Elecan't?" Lily asked.

"Why, I'm going right back to the circus," the Elecan't shouted. "There's no need for me to run away now. I'm going to move big logs. I'm going to fling big rocks. I am going to help put up the big top just like the others do."

The Elecan't raised his terrific new trunk.

"And I am going to trumpet music to the heavens with this tooter like the world has never heard before."

With that the Elecan't departed, thanking his friends for the enormous favor they had done for him. He waddled from the Great Green Forest as the rays of the full moon lit his way back to the circus.

Two days later, Freddie ran to Lily's tree with a newspaper. On the front page was a picture of the Elecan't raising his trunk as an adoring crowd cheered. The headline read:

TRUMPETING ELEPHANT SAVES CIRCUS!
WARNS ANIMALS AS FIRE DESTROYS THE BIG TOP

The article below explained how the little elephant returned to the circus late that night after visiting some woodland friends and arrived just in time to discover a fire had broken out while everyone slept. The little elephant sounded the alarm as his tooter filled the night sky with blaring trumpet blasts and generous gobs of gray-green gobbledygook. His quick action awakened everyone and saved a hundred lives. The Big Top tent was also saved by this little elephant that showed the other elephants how to fill their trunks with water like hoses and douse the fire. As a result of this little elephant's bravery, the circus was saved.

"Look at this," Lily read. "They are calling him an elephant now, and a hero."

"No more Elecan't," Freddie grinned. "He's made the big time."

Indeed, many of the hero's fellow circus friends were quoted in the paper, and each stated what a wonderful little elephant they thought he was and how they knew when he was just a baby that the little elephant would grow to be something special.

Oh, the story is not quite over, even though the happy ending has already been told. For you see, Einstein never stretched the Elecan't trunk all that much. He just pretended the tiny trunk was stretching in the moonlight. For wise Einstein gave the Elecan't something much more precious than a longer trunk to brag about that night. The owl taught the Elecan't that *anyone* can do amazing things with what was naturally given to them if they just believed in themselves and trusted their own judgment. And you know, that's just about all that anyone could ask of anyone.

CHAPTER 15

LILY'S TWINKLE

One cold winter's day, Lily looked around the Great Green Forest, now thoroughly white with snow, and said, "You know, I like my home, but I would like to see something other than snow."

It was, after all, winter and Lily had watched snow fall week after week. It seemed as if the snowfall was going to go on forever, and Lily grew weary of seeing nothing but snow. *If white was all I wanted to see,* she thought, *I may as well sit in front of a mirror all day.* Lily visited Honest Bob's Trading Post and Travel Agency on the far side of the Great Green Forest. She found out about a place where Honest Bob assured her, through nervous twitches of his whiskers, that there was very little snow to get in her way of having fun. After all, Lily concluded, a pack rat with a name like Honest Bob wouldn't ever tell anyone any sort of fib about the weather. But she sure wondered how the pack rat had procured the scar on the left side of his nose. Lily got a ride to the airport with Bruno the Badger's Carriage and Sky Taxi Service and had great fun being pulled by a team of bats flying high in the air above her, even though she knew bats couldn't see their own noses in the daylight. Lily then snuck inside a plane Bruno told her about and flew over miles and miles of water. In fact, after a while, Lily was beginning to wonder if she would ever see land again. She had no idea the big round world she lived on contained so much water. But the plane finally passed over land once more and after a few more hours landed safely on the ground. Lily snuck back out of the plane and looked around. Honest Bob had been right. This place had hardly any snow at all. In fact, it didn't have a whole lot of anything. This was nothing like the Great Green Forest, and the strangeness of it all made her feel a bit uneasy. But this strange land sure had a lot of rocks. There were rocks all over the place—big rocks, little rocks, and even medium-sized rocks. As she walked among them, they hurt Lily's tender little squirrel feet, so she learned to be very careful where she stepped. Lily tied a red knapsack with all her chocolate peanut clusters inside onto the end of a big wooden stick and hung it over her shoulder. She found a path and began to walk, amazed at how far she could see without any trees in the way. Lily had no idea where she was going and wondered if Honest Bob had really been honest with her about this place. Lily walked for hours until the sun began to set, lighting up the sky with bright colors of reds and oranges as it slipped below the horizon. As it grew dark, Lily suddenly realized she didn't know where she was or where she was going to sleep that night. But there was absolutely no one around to ask. *Perhaps she should have planned a bit better*, she thought.

Lily walked in the darkness for a while as the stars began to appear in the sky above her. They twinkled and seemed to be winking at her as if they knew something she didn't. She remembered her mother used to say Lily had a twinkle in her eyes much brighter than any of the stars in the heavens. Lily always appreciated her mother's compliment, for some of the stars above her shone quite brightly. But her mother said hers shone the brightest of them all. She looked up to the sky as she walked; wink–twinkle–wink–twinkle–wink–twinkle–wink went the stars.

Lily became so engrossed in their beauty she failed to notice that in the dark she wandered off the path.

BAMM!

Lily ran smack into something hard and tumbled to the ground. For a moment she saw a lot more stars than she wanted to see, and some of them spun rapidly around her head. And they were a lot closer than the ones in the sky. Lily looked up to see what she had smashed up against.

It was a signpost and it read, "Bethlehem," and below it were painted the words, "Just a little farther down the road."

This is great, Lily thought, as she shook the spinning stars from her head. Now she could find a place to stay and to munch on her chocolate peanut clusters. She needed to find somewhere warm, for she could feel the night air was getting cooler. Lily was thankful her white fur grew thick to protect her from the weather. She often wondered how humans survived the cold with their thin, almost worthless skin wrapped around their bodies. They might as well have been wearing the skin of an onion for all the good theirs did. But that was their problem and not hers. The little squirrel walked past the signpost and came upon a little hut in a gentle-rolling valley. In the dim light of a candle shining through a window, Lily saw a man and a beautiful woman watching a little baby lying in a wooden box. The baby had only a little shawl wrapped around it for protection against the cold. The baby was crying. Lily listened as the man spoke to the woman.

"If we cannot keep the baby warm," the man said in a worried voice, "he will surely perish in the cold."

"Yes," the woman fretted, "but I have nothing else to give him to keep him warm."

The man stood tall and put his arm around the woman. He spoke gently to her.

"We must have faith that all things will be given."

Boy, Lily thought. *And I thought I had a problem.* Lily watched the little baby shivering inside the cold wooden box and then looked down at her own warm white coat of fur. Her little heart fluttered as she realized what she must do. Lily jumped through the window and landed on the dirt floor inside of the hut.

"Look!" the man shouted, his loud voice frightening Lily.

As Lily approached the wooden box where the little baby lay, the man picked up a big stick, for he thought the squirrel was going to bite his newborn child. Perhaps, in this strange land, this man had never seen a squirrel before.

"Wait," the beautiful woman cautioned, holding back the man's arm as he was about to take a swing at Lily. Then she looked into his eyes and repeated the man's own words back to him. "We must have faith that all things will be given."

The man and woman watched as Lily climbed over the side of the wooden box and covered the baby with her own warm coat of fur. She had lots of soft white fur and it filled the wooden box to the top. The baby murmured at first, but was soon sleeping soundly because of the warmth Lily provided. Lily found it to be very warm in the wooden box, and she too fell asleep, tired after her own long journey.

Two hours later Lily felt a hand on her and woke. She looked up and saw the beautiful woman shaking her.

"It is time for me to feed the baby, Little Friend," she said to Lily. She smiled. "Your warmth has saved him."

The woman pulled the sleeping infant from beneath the little squirrel's fur. Lily looked around and saw a host of others gathered around the hut. Lily saw some people, some goats, some sheep, a couple of camels, a donkey, and a dog looking through the window of the hut, and her heart leapt. *The circus was in town! Perhaps tomorrow*, Lily thought, *she could walk into Bethlehem and see all those animals perform their acts.* And she wondered what kind of tricks a goat or a sheep could be taught to do. While the woman fed the baby, Lily decided to go outside and look at the night sky. The stars were still winking and twinkling down at her. Lily watched the stars for a while and then spied an old man with a white beard sitting alone on a craggy rock near the hut. She went over to talk to him and saw his eyes were very sad.

"Who are you?" Lily asked.

"I'm the baby's father," the old man answered.

Lily thought about what he said and scratched her head. You see she was a little confused by this. Then she pointed back at the hut with her little paw.

"Now wait a minute," she exclaimed. "I'm a bit mixed up here. I thought that guy in the hut was the baby's father."

"It gets a little complicated right here, Lily," the old man said. "We kind of both are."

"You both are the father?" Lily asked, puzzled by the man's words. "This baby has two dads?" Lily grew even more confused now. "By the way, how do you know my name is Lily? And you don't seem to be surprised to see a squirrel here in this land where they are not supposed to be. I find that most odd."

"I know everybody's name," the old man replied. "That's just a trick I know. And an animal or a bird or a plant is wherever it happens to be found. The rules about where they're supposed to live are a bit fluid, you understand."

"Well, I can see that," Lily agreed. "But what's going on here tonight?"

He looked at Lily. "What if I were to tell you, Lily, what's taking place right now might have actually happened a long time ago? What would you say about that?"

"I'd say you own some powerful magic," Lily replied. "Dragging the past into present, that is."

"Perhaps what you are witnessing this evening happened, as I said, a long time ago," the old man explained. "And it's much more powerful than any magic. You are wiser than you think in saying what you just said. You got lucky, squirrel. Tonight we took the show on the road and you get to be a part of it. You picked a good night to visit."

"I'm a bit confused," Lily answered, scratching her head. "But you seem like a man of wisdom so I'll play along."

The man smiled and then spoke. "But... about your other question, about the two-dad dilemma. Don't worry about that—it's just sort of a deal we worked out between us to help get the job done, more as a matter of convenience for all parties. Understand, Lily?"

Lily scratched her head.

"Not really," she replied. "But it must be some kind of job that needs to be done."

"Indeed, it is," the old man explained. "It involves many players and many pieces. If you don't understand that, then I guess it's a little early to tell you about some other things I know about. Letting you know stuff like building walls of water and making things out of nothing would mess with your head. I tell you what, Lily, just forget I mentioned all this for now. I have a much bigger problem to fix at this time."

"What's that?" Lily asked, her mind trying to comprehend what a wall made from water would look like and why a wall would need to be made of water if it was supposed to keep people from peeking in at you. His words made little sense to her.

"Nothing you can help me with, I'm afraid," the old man replied.

"Tell me, please," Lily urged. "What have you got to lose?"

The old man thought for a minute and then spoke.

"I guess you're right on that point, Lily," he agreed. "I guess I should learn to trust my creatures a little more. They're often much more reliable than these humans you see running around here. He stroked his beard. "You see, my little squirrel friend, there are three guys who are supposed to come by tonight to see that new baby in there. These guys are big shots, and I had in mind they would be here tonight when I wrote the script."

"Wrote the script?" Lily asked. She was really confused now.

"Never mind," the old man replied. "Just a little celestial humor."

"Well, just tell them to get on over here," Lily said. "That's simple."

"Well," the old man explained, rubbing one hand over his mouth. "I wish it were that simple. You see, I told them to follow a special light in the sky. It was to be in the form of a star with a special super-duper twinkle."

The old man looked up at the heavens.

"But I guess I forgot just how many stars I put up there," he said. "I probably should have been a little more specific with my directions." He looked around and drew close to Lily, whispering. "They say I'm sometimes too much of a control freak." He chuckled. "And maybe they have a point."

Lily didn't understand what the old man was trying to tell her, but she offered a solution to his problem.

"Why don't you just give one of those stars up there one of your super-duper twinkles," she suggested. "Wouldn't that solve the problem? I mean look at them sprinkled all over up there."She pointed to one star almost directly overhead.

"How about that one over there? Then it would be easy to follow."

"I have already thought about that," the old man said. "Unfortunately, there are laws around here prohibiting working on certain days and this happens to be one of them. And it is a little late at night to go out shopping for a super-duper twinkler. The retail shopping laws in this part of the world are strict with their hours of operation, and a super-duper twinkler is hard enough to find even if the stores were still open. You can see my dilemma now, Lily. No twinkler, no big shot visitors."

Lily suddenly thought of something.

"You know, my mother once told me I have a twinkle in my eyes much brighter than any star in the heavens. And my mother always told me the truth."

The old man looked straight into Lily's eyes.

"Wow, Lily," he said admiringly. "That is indeed quite a twinkling twinkler you have there. I guess I was so caught up with my own needs I failed to see what you bring to the table." He stared at Lily's eyes now, fascinated. "That twinkler of yours would light up the night sky if it was hanging up there." Then he smiled. "Friend Lily, would you consider loaning me the twinkle in your eyes? I'll make sure to give it back to you when I'm done with it."

"I would be most happy to let you borrow my twinkle," Lily answered. "It would be my pleasure, and I'm sure my mother would be proud of me for doing it."

She pointed at the sky high above them.

"But how would you get it way up there? It's got to be at least a couple of hundred feet up to all those stars," she guessed. "Can you jump that high? No disrespect intended, Sir, but you *are* an old man, after all."

"That would not be a problem," the old man assured her. "There are some things I am quite good at doing, even as an old man. I actually get things right most of the time, believe it or not."

"I have no reason to doubt you," Lily said. "Although I have just met you, I feel I have known you forever." The old man gave her a knowing smile and she pointed to her eyes. "Kindly take my twinkle then, old man, for the sake of the baby."

"Okay, I will," the old man said. "And it is with a grateful heart that I take your twinkle. But first, close your eyes, friend Lily."

Lily closed her eyes as the old man asked and felt his hands gently touch her eyes. When she opened them again, her vision was blurry at first but cleared as she looked up at the sky. She immediately spotted a bright new twinkle lighting up the night sky in the east. The twinkle was brighter than any star shining in the heavens. Lily smiled at the old man.

"Your three friends should be able to see that," Lily said. "They'd have to be blind not to."

"The light will pierce the darkness," the old man smiled, carefully choosing his words. "And even the blind shall see."

Lily and the old man heard footsteps behind them. Someone approached them from the shadows. It was the man from the hut. He, too, looked up at the sky and admired the new twinkle.

"That's my twinkle up there," Lily said proudly. "It will guide your three friends to this place."

The man from the hut looked over at the old man sitting on the rock, as if puzzled by what Lily told him. The old man raised his hand and nodded his head, perhaps warning the man not to read too much into what the little squirrel said.

"The baby is fed, my friend," the man from the hut told Lily. "Would you mind coming back in and lending us your warmth again? The baby does so love it and badly needs his sleep."

"Gladly," Lily replied. "It would be my pleasure."

Before they left, the old man leaned over and whispered something into Lily's ear.

"Do you suppose I can keep your twinkle until tomorrow morning?" he asked. "I promise to give it back to you then. These three big shots are generally pretty smart guys, but apparently not so much tonight. I asked them to take horses, but I fear they're on camels. They like to show off by riding way up in the air, and camels allow them to do that better than horses do. Apparently, vanity trumps common sense this evening, and they might be running a little late. But I'm sure they'll get here sometime tonight."

"That's right," Lily reminded him, not understanding the words she spoke or why she was saying them now. "Because, as you said earlier, you wrote the script."

Then she told him something else.

"Besides," she said, "something tells me if I can't trust you, I can't trust anyone."

"That's very comforting to know," the old man said as a smile appeared on his face. "Wish more people thought that way."

Lily returned to warm the baby with her fur all through the cold night. The next morning, she found the old man was gone, and to her surprise, her twinkle was still shining in the sky high above them. That worried her, for it meant she had no twinkle in her eyes and she dearly wanted her twinkle back. But, just as the old man had promised, his three friends had arrived on camels.They were Fancy Men! And they wore fancy clothes! Lily watched the three men place some pieces of metal and smelly stuff on the ground near the wooden box. *Some friends*, Lily thought, remembering what the old man had said about them. *Look at all this junk. Why didn't they at least bring the kid a few chocolate peanut clusters? You can't eat metal, and babies certainly didn't need any smelly stuff. They smell pretty good all by themselves.* One of the Fancy Men handed Lily something.

"Here, Little Squirrel," the Fancy Man said. "I found this in my saddlebag this morning. I don't know where it came from, but you can have it. I don't like nuts."

"Maybe the old man put it there," Lily suggested.

"What old man?" the Fancy Man asked.

Lily took the strange package, wrapped in the kind of special paper made for a king. She opened it and found a chocolate peanut cluster, Lily's favorite food. Lily was so hungry she took a big bite of the candy. Then she felt a funny tingling in her eyes. She looked toward the sky where her twinkle had been and now saw it was gone.

"Wow!" the Fancy Man said, watching her munch. "That stuff really puts a twinkle into your eyes."

Lily thought about what the Fancy Man said and glanced over to see her reflection in a nearby puddle. Her twinkle shone like a bright star in the field of blue water. She knew something wonderful happened during the night and she had played an important role in bringing a happy ending to the story. And that satisfaction, along with a bit of help from the chocolate peanut cluster, left a very good taste in her mouth.

CHAPTER 16

LILY AND MONTEZUMA THE MONKEY

Elvis is a toucan, a very beautiful and colorful bird, and he will tell that to any creature in the Great Green Forest, even if they don't want to hear about what a magnificent sight he is to behold. Indeed, it is a fact once Elvis gets to talking, there's no shutting him up. There are two things Elvis likes about himself. The first is the flowing shock of black hair that drapes over the top of his head. How many birds do you know that have a shock of hair, or any other hair for that matter? The other thing Elvis likes about himself is his long yellow beak. Everyone who wants to find Elvis just looks for his beak first, and when they find the flash of yellow, they know Elvis is somewhere right behind it.

One day Lily was walking through one of the many trails weaving through the Great Green Forest and strolled past a small magnolia tree. Just as Lily was about to walk by the tree, she spied something on the lowest branch of the tree.

"Oh," Lily said in a surprised voice. "It's a banana! How strange, considering this is a magnolia tree and bananas don't grow on magnolia trees."

But in the Great Green Forest, the Forest Wizard sometimes worked magic not everyone understood, and Lily reminded herself of that. The

Wizard was also prone to pulling pranks once in a while. He might have waved his wizard wand and POOF—bananas suddenly hung from a magnolia tree.

"I bet," she said smiling, "the Forest Wizard made the banana grow on the magnolia tree so someone alert enough to see it would get the banana as a prize."

Lily figured since she had been clever enough to see the banana, she deserved to eat it before someone else found it. Lily walked under the umbrella of thick magnolia leaves and reached her paw up to pick the banana. Just as she was about to put her paw around the fruit, she heard a sound like someone snoring, and she stopped to look around. As her eyes grew accustomed to the shadow of the tree, she saw the banana was hanging not from a branch, but from something very black. Lily took a step closer to the tree and found the banana was being held in the tree by a bunch of black feathers.

"Very strange," Lily noted, as she studied the feathers.

Then Lily watched as the feathers moved slowly up and down. She heard the snoring again and realized it came from somewhere in those feathers.

"My stars," Lily whispered in amazement. "That isn't a banana at all! It's Elvis the Toucan Bird, napping soundly as if he didn't have a care in the world. What a silly little squirrel I have been to think a beak could be a banana."

Deep in Lily's brain sat an extremely spongy ball of yellow goop where squirrels store their mischief. It's right next to the thinking part, but a tad lower and to the left. When Lily's thinking part and mischief part got together, Lily sometimes came up with wonderful ideas, ones that ought not to go to waste. Lily slowly pulled back from the thick-leafed magnolia tree, ever so careful not to make a sound to wake Elvis. She turned and ran from the forest and took the back way into a city. It proved to be quite a journey, but eventually she found herself at the zoo and in front of the cage of her monkey friend Montezuma.

"Hello, Lily," Montezuma said happily. "I haven't seen you here in a long time."

"Hello, Montezuma," Lily said with a smile. "I have to be careful when I come here. I don't want to end up in there like you—no offense."

"None taken," the monkey replied. "You like the woods. I like the zoo. There are a lot of advantages to being here. You never go hungry. You never have to worry about getting eaten. You always have a warm bed—they give us clean straw every day. You're never caught out in the rain. And humans who visit here take my picture when I show off for them. Yes, Lily, you like being in the woods and I like being in the zoo."

"But I have found something wonderful in the forest for you," Lily explained. "Something made just for a monkey. Something super scrumptious. I have come to ask if you want to have it."

"What is it?" Montezuma asked, his curiosity aroused. "What could you possibly have in the forest that would interest me?"

Montezuma thought there would be very little in the forest he would be interested in unless Lily had finally found the perfect branch he could wrap his tail around and hang down from. It was every monkey's dream to find a perfect tail-curler branch, but few ever had done it. But Montezuma figured if Lily had found a perfect tail curler, he would be the envy of every other monkey at the zoo.

"You will have to come with me and I will show you," Lily explained.

"Tell me what it is and I will come," Montezuma said.

"No," Lily said, "that would spoil the surprise."

"Okay, I'll go," the monkey agreed. "I guess I could *hang* around with you for a bit." The monkey hoped his clue would trigger the squirrel to give away her secret about finding the perfect tail-curler branch, but it did no such thing. He continued. "But how will I get out of this cage?"

"Leave that to me," Lily instructed, climbing to the top of the cage and flicking her tail down toward the monkey. "Now wrap your tail around my tail, and I will pull you up."

Montezuma did as Lily told him, and soon the monkey and the squirrel were dashing off into the forest. They didn't stop running until they stood before the little magnolia tree.

"I knew it!" Montezuma exclaimed. "Lily, you have found the perfect tail curler!"

Now Lily had no idea what a perfect tail curler was let alone what it was supposed to look like.

"No, Montezuma," she explained. "It's nothing like that." She pointed. "Look underneath that branch."

Montezuma moved beneath the canopy of green leaves and looked up at what Lily pointed toward. In front of him, the monkey saw the most enormous banana he had ever seen in his life! His eyes widened and he heard his stomach growling like a lion. It begged for that banana. All thoughts of finding a perfect tail curler disappeared as his stomach growled once more.

"See, I told you I had a surprise," Lily said.

Then Lily turned her head away, faking a cough so Montezuma wouldn't see the wide grin on her face.

"Thank you, Lily!" Montezuma said, reaching for the banana. "I wish my zookeeper was here to see how quickly I will snatch up this banana. He always tells me I'd starve without him and that's why he feeds me. He says I've been out of the jungle too long and I've lost my mojo, whatever that is. I'll just show him now. And I'll take this fine banana back with me to show him what's what."

Before Lily could tell the monkey it was all a joke, Montezuma leaned in and grabbed Elvis' beak and prepared to take a bite. Then he gave Lily a thumb's up.

"Ooh, this is going to taste super good," he said. "Just wait until I show this to my nasty old zookeeper."

Elvis woke up to find his beak caught in something. In the dark events had gotten very confusing.

"Awk," Elvis said, in a muffled squawk, because he couldn't open his mouth to say anything more.

Needless to say, Montezuma became quite surprised to find his banana was talking back at him as he was trying to pry it off the magnolia tree. He saw a pair of eyes staring at him from directly above the banana. He jerked his body backward.

"Why, you're not a banana at all!" he said indignantly. "You're Elvis the Toucan Bird!"

"I have never been and will never be a banana!" Elvis shouted back. The toucan fluttered from his perch and landed on another branch a few feet away. "And you are a monkey with very bad eyesight! Don't you know bananas don't grow on magnolia trees?"

Then they heard Lily laughing at them and turned to look at her."Ha-ha-ha," Lily laughed. "A monkey who can't tell a banana from a bird's beak. Ha-ha-ha."

"Darn you, Lily," Montezuma scolded. "You tricked me, didn't you? This was all a joke from the beginning, wasn't it?"

"And you woke me up from a very fine nap," Elvis snapped, not at all happy with Lily.

Lily continued to laugh.

"I'm sorry, friends," she said. "Please don't be angry with me. I just couldn't pass up the chance to play a trick on you. Please don't be mad at me."

Elvis thought about what just happened and realized how funny it must have looked. Now it was his turn to laugh.

"Okay, Lily," he chuckled. "You are right. It was a good joke. A very funny joke indeed."

But Montezuma said nothing to Lily. He was too busy staring at something in the magnolia tree.

"Now don't be mad at me, Montezuma," Lily pleaded. "I was just having some fun. Nobody got hurt."

But still the monkey looked into the tree and said nothing.

"What's he looking at?" Elvis whispered to Lily.

"I don't know," Lily replied.

Montezuma's attention was elsewhere at the moment, for the monkey had spotted something at the exact spot Elvis had perched when they'd arrived at the tree. The branch where the toucan rested was worn shiny and smooth because Elvis' feet had gripped and polished the same spot hundreds of times while he napped. The branch was a monkey's holy grail and Montezuma knew it. The shining branch held his attention as if the monkey were hypnotized.

"What is it, Montezuma?" Lily asked him. "What is so interesting in the tree?"

With his monkey instincts fully engaged now, Montezuma knew what he'd seen. But he couldn't be sure unless he tried it himself. He pointed to the smooth branch Elvis had been resting on and chattered excitedly.

"T-t-t-ta-ta-ta-aiil-cur-r-rler! Tail curler!"

The monkey scurried up the tree and curled his tail firmly around the branch. The wood was still warm from the toucan's body, and it fit the monkey's tail perfectly.

"Ooh-ooh-aah-aah," he said with a tone of immense pleasure. "Ooooh-oo and a double aah-aah. Man, this is living."

The monkey looked over at the squirrel and the bird. Then he slid his rear end over the branch and eased his body down. His tail now bore all his weight as he dangled above the ground.

"Tail curler!" he shouted with glee as his body shook the magnolia leaves, "Tail curler! Look at me, everyone!"

"I don't know what he's doing," Elvis said to Lily. "But I'm pretty sure he's going to forgive you for playing that trick on him."

Montezuma hung on the branch for the better part of an hour, his eyes closed as if he were in heaven, his body pushed back and forth by a breeze. Lily scurried to the Big Oak and got her camera and took lots of pictures of Montezuma as he hung there as content as a monkey could be.

When Montezuma finally came down from the tree, his little tail was sore from being curled up for such a long time. Lily took him back to the zoo and gave him the pictures she had taken. The monkey showed the zookeeper the picture of Elvis' beak, leaving out the part about it not being a banana. The zookeeper was forced to admit Montezuma could, indeed, forage for his own food if circumstances forced him to. As a result, the zookeeper promised not to tease the monkey so much since a monkey who could find his own food would put any zookeeper out of a job.

Montezuma has pretty much forgotten he ever tried to eat Elvis' beak because he mistook it for his favorite food. He's too busy being popular with all the other monkeys in the zoo. For Montezuma is the only one among them ever to find the perfect tail curler.

And he has the pictures to prove it.

CHAPTER 17

LILY AND THE KANGAROO FROM KOOKABURRA

One morning Lily woke up and opened the itty-bitty door of her house in the trunk of the Big Oak. Below her front door, the great big branch stretched out, and on the branch, green moss grew like soft carpet. *That branch looks like a tightrope*, she thought. She imagined herself as a circus tightrope walker and began walking along the branch, one leg at a time. Although the branch was thicker than a tightrope, Lily imagined the branch was thin as one would be, and therefore her heart thumped with excitement over the peril existing only in the little squirrel's head. That's the wonderful thing about imagination. It takes you to places you might never visit and dangers you may never experience, and it may be just as well those dangers remain stored safely in one's head.

Now about the time Lily made her way to the end of the branch, Elvis the Toucan Bird landed on the branch just above her. Elvis was sometimes very mischievous, and as he watched Lily walking along the branch, he thought of a trick he could play. After all, since Lily recently played a trick on him with a monkey named Montezuma, Elvis figured he owed the squirrel a prank. He opened his big banana beak and squawked.

"A-a-a-a-w-w-w-a-a-kkk!" he cried and then roared with laughter as he watched Lily jump into the air.

Well Lily hadn't been expecting anything like this, and the loud screech startled her. Lily was right in the middle of a step, so she was standing on one leg, and when she heard the loud squawk from Elvis, she lost her balance when she jumped up and she tumbled over the side of the branch. Elvis peered over his branch and watched Lily fall.

"Oops," he said. "That didn't go well."

Elvis thought it would be better if he just got out of there while the getting was good. Off he flew and down fell Lily. *This is going to hurt*, she thought as she saw the ground below her. She closed her eyes, waiting to feel the hard thump when she hit the ground. But instead, she fell onto something very soft. Lily opened her eyes and found it was very dark. *Perhaps she had died and gone to Squirrel Heaven*, she thought at first but then pinched herself and, to her great relief, discovered she was still among the living. But then another thought came to her.

"Oh, no!" she shouted, "I can't see! I've gone blind!"

But a small ray of light shined upon her from above, and the squirrel saw that instead of being blind, she was surrounded by what seemed to be a mountain of hairy brown fur. It was very warm in this dark place, and it smelled a bit like Robert the Moose's wet fur after a hard rain. Lily managed to turn around in this dark place and bumped into something. Click-click-click, came the sound, click-click-click. Lily discovered she had bumped into a leather bag and it clicked at her. *Why would a leather bag click?* She slapped her paw at the pouch again, and once more she heard click-click-click. Then her dark place began to shake very hard, and she heard a voice coming from above her.

"Ha-ha-ha," the voice laughed. "Ha-ha! Stop it!"

Lily spied a slit-shaped light above her and poked her head up through the darkness and into the light. A big head, the likes of which she'd never encountered before, was the source of the laughter. Lots of brown fur covered the rest of the beast. Gathering her wits, Lily realized she had fallen into the soft pouch of this strange animal. Because of this, her life had been saved.

"Who are you?" Lily demanded. "Better yet, what are you? I know all the animals in the Great Green Forest, but I've never seen the likes of you here before."

"That's because I'm not from the Great Green Forest," the animal replied. "I'm merely here on a mission. And I'm a kangaroo, if you must know. And you have fallen into my pouch. You should be grateful I happened along." The kangaroo laughed once more. "Ha-ha-ha. Now you're tickling me, Little Squirrel."

"It's Lily," Lily replied, somewhat flustered. "My name is Lily and I'm not tickling you."

"Oh, yes you are," the kangaroo argued. "Your little feet are tickling the inside of my pouch."

"Well, how could you tell?" Lily shot back. "Your pouch is full of junk."

"Junk!" the kangaroo exclaimed. "Are you daring to call my pouch a garbage can?"

"Yes," Lily defended. "There's a big bag of something in there going click-click-click."

"Oh," the kangaroo answered. "My stars, Lily the Squirrel, that's not junk—no-no-no, not now or not ever. That's my other pouch inside my pouch. It's my pouch full of wonderful and colorful marbles."

"Marbles!" Lily shouted. "Why would a kangaroo carry around a pouch full of marbles? I'm sure you can't eat them."

"Perhaps I should introduce myself first, Lily," he replied. "You see I am the famous Kangaroo from Kookaburra—*the* Kangaroo from Kookaburra, that is. Not to be confused with the common kangaroos living there."

"And where, pray tell, is this Kookaburra?" Lily asked. "I've never heard of it or ever seen it on a map."

"Well," said the kangaroo, pointing, "you just go south about as far as you can go, and then go just a little bit further, and then scoot east and you'll find Kookaburra. If you get lost, just ask anybody you run into. They'll all know and most likely chide you for not knowing where it is in the first place."

"I'll try to remember that," Lily answered, jumping from the kangaroo's pouch and onto the ground. "But what is it about you that makes you as famous as you say you are?"

"Ah, little squirrel," the Kangaroo from Kookaburra answered, "I am also the best marble shooter in the whole world, that's all. But Kookaburra didn't make me famous. I made *it* famous."

"The best marble shooter in the whole world?" Lily asked. "That's quite a mouthful. With a front pouch to boot."

"Well," the kangaroo chuckled, "I don't know whether you are aware of this or not, since you've never met a kangaroo before today, but pouches are a luxury only female kangaroos have to carry their little joeys, or babies. I have no idea why baby kangaroos are called joeys, but they are. I had this pouch installed merely as a convenience, and I use it exclusively to carry my marbles. That is the only reason I have it at all. As silly as a pouch may seem on a male kangaroo, I find it just as silly to be talking to a white squirrel. Aren't you little creatures supposed to be brown or gray or some other drab color?"

"Well," Lily explained, "the fact of the matter is, my mother told me I was born brown, but then a baby tornado came through my house and whirled snow all over me and changed my fur from brown to white."

"Sure it did," the kangaroo snickered. "That's a good one. At least my pouch story is true. Baby tornado and a snow-dyed squirrel indeed! Ha!"

The Kangaroo from Kookaburra looked at Lily's little white face.

"But in three days, I will be a champion. Just three measly days from now."

"You will be what in three days?" Lily asked. "And why are you here in the Great Green Forest?"

"I am here in the Great Green Forest because it is the quickest way for me to get to the Open Meadow," the Kangaroo from Kookaburra explained. "That is where the World Marble Shooting Tournament is going to take place. In three days, I will be the World Marble Shooting Champion. That is why I'm here, and that is why I had this pouch installed. I'm a marble shooter, and I have to carry my bag of marbles around when I compete. What better way to keep your paws free than to store all these heavy marbles in a pouch." The kangaroo sat back on his tail and raised his paws like a boxer. "See, Lily, my paws are free to take on anyone who wants to bother me."

"You are here to become the World Marble Shooting Champion?" Lily asked. "You mean you aren't already?"

"No," the Kangaroo from Kookaburra replied in a miffed tone. "I have never been able to beat Ollie the Ostrich—drat him. He has beaten me five straight years in a row. But I think I've discovered a way to beat that oversized pigeon this time around."

"I hope you beat him then," Lily said. "May I go with you and watch? I know the forest well, and I can help you get to the Open Meadow. If you need anything, I can fetch it for you during your tournament. I know all the shortcuts through the woods."

"I would love to have some company, Lily the Squirrel," the Kangaroo from Kookaburra replied. "I have traveled a long way and I have been lonely, and sometimes all I have to listen to is the sound of marbles clicking against each other in my pouch. That click-click-click will drive you nuts after a while."

"I'm a bit of an expert on nuts myself," Lily said. "I can just imagine that constant racket would make you a bit nutty."

"And did I mention I was born during a leap year," the kangaroo added.

"I just bet you were," Lily replied, looking at the kangaroo's thick legs.

"But most kangaroos are, you know," the kangaroo agreed. "It's not a big deal."

"And probably most rabbits," Lily added. "If you really think about it."

The kangaroo shot Lily a quizzical look as if it never dawned on him those lowly creatures called rabbits were born during a leap year just like kangaroos. He made a mental note when he got back to Kookaburra to check and see if what the squirrel proposed could somehow be true. He couldn't comprehend how some shaggy little rodent like a common rabbit could be born in a leap year. A leap year should be reserved for the large and majestic kangaroo family and not for lowly rabbits.

Lily and the Kangaroo from Kookaburra began their long trek to the Open Meadow. The kangaroo picked Lily up and placed her on his shoulder while they walked. They talked about many things as all the while the marbles went click-click-click deep in the kangaroo's pouch. When they arrived at the Open Meadow later, they found lots of animals had come to compete in the tournament. Elephants and monkeys, penguins and seals, flamingoes and hyenas, and all sorts of other animals traveled from far away to the Open Meadow to shoot marbles. In the middle of the meadow, a large crowd gathered and listened with rapture to a rather large bird. The bird was talking very loudly and waving his wings around with dramatic flair.

"Who's that?" Lily asked.

"That is Ollie the Ostrich," the Kangaroo from Kookaburra answered with distain. "He's the oversized pigeon I told you about. He's also a big windbag. I must beat him this year just so I won't have to listen to him crowing yet again about how he's the best marble shooter in the world. It really annoys me."

"How come he wins all the time?" Lily asked. "What's his secret?"

"It's his beak," the Kangaroo from Kookaburra replied. "Watch him when the tournament begins and you'll see."

That night all the animals sat in a huge circle around a gigantic campfire and feasted on all kinds of food. Some of the animals stood up and told stories, and of course Ollie the Ostrich reminded everyone he had won the last five marble shooting tournaments and intended to make it six. Finally, the Grand Master Walrus, who oversaw the competition, stood up and spoke to the crowd.

"Greetings, friends," he began. "We are so very glad you have traveled from all over the world to the Open Meadow to compete in the World Marble Shooting Tournament. Play fair and shoot your very best for the next three days. Be kind to each other and be good sports whether you win or don't win. Our prize for the winner this year is forty-five pounds of goodies—whatever goodies the winner chooses from the World Marble Shooting Tournament Goodie Bin."

"Forty-five pounds of goodies!" Lily exclaimed excitedly, licking her lips. "Imagine how happy I would be with forty-five pounds of chocolate peanut clusters. Why, I'd have to get Freddie the Indian to help me carry all those goodies back to my house. But, on second thought, I'm quite sure my little house isn't big enough to hold so much."

"Now everyone had better go to sleep and get a good night's rest," the Grand Master Walrus suggested. "For tomorrow will be a very busy day and all marble shooters will need to be at their very best."

The next day the Official Tournament Rooster, wearing a beautiful red ribbon around his neck, crowed precisely as dawn broke, and all the animals quickly sprang from their place of rest. The World Marble Shooting Tournament began immediately following breakfast. The Open Meadow was divided into twenty-seven circles, and all sorts of animals shot into the circles, trying to knock their opponents' marbles out of the game. When one contestant managed to knock an opponent's five marbles from the circle, the winner would play another opponent after a quick break for spearmint juice and cookies. It took three full days of marble shooting, from dawn to shortly after dusk, for the hundreds and hundreds of contestants to finish playing. When they had all played, only two marble shooters had not lost a single contest. The World Marble Shooting Tournament Championship would boil down to Ollie the Ostrich and the Kangaroo from Kookaburra, just as the kangaroo predicted it would.

"Well, Kangaroo from Kookaburra," Ollie the Ostrich teased, "why don't you just pack those cute little marbles of yours up and go on home now. Stash them in that smelly old pouch of yours and hop on back to Loser Land where you belong. You know I'm only going to beat you once again."

The Kangaroo from Kookaburra remained silent but hung his head. He had lost to the ostrich five times already. The words the ostrich spoke cut into his very heart.

"No, you won't!" Lily shouted at Ollie, her voice firm and deliberate. "The Kangaroo from Kookaburra will beat you this time, you overgrown pigeon!"

Lily immediately regretted her unkind words because the Grand Master Walrus told everyone to be kind and good sports. But Lily was angered by the bird's treatment of the kangaroo.

"Yea, yea, yea," Ollie answered sarcastically. "I've heard that story many times before. I'll tell you what, little white rat... oops—I mean squirrel, if the kangaroo beats me, I will personally allow you to pluck out my grandest tail feather."

He pointed to a magnificent feather sprouting from his tail and wiggled his rear end to show it off. The feather waving in the breeze was colorful and majestic and much longer than any of the other feathers in his tail.

"I'll take that bet," Lily shot back. "If the kangaroo loses, you may pluck out one of my whiskers." The ostrich studied Lily's face, eyeing the squirrel's fine long whiskers. "I think I'll take that bet as well, squirrel. Your whisker would make an excellent toothpick."

Lily turned to the kangaroo. "Do your best, Kangaroo. You have already beaten so many great marble shooters from around the world. You've beaten everyone you've faced. Don't think less of yourself because of one blowhard bird. You need to be confident now. You can beat him. I know you can."

Hundreds of birds and animals huddled around the circle as the kangaroo and the ostrich prepared to play the championship match. Each of them put five of their best marbles in the middle of the circle. Ollie used smoky-black marbles with swirls of white inside. The Kangaroo from Kookaburra used clear marbles with blue and red swirls. Each animal selected their favorite shooter, a fat marble much bigger than the smaller marbles they placed inside the circle.

Now, since Ollie was the defending champion, he shot first. The crowd clamored as Ollie's shooter marble hit one of the kangaroo's marbles squarely and bounced it out of the circle.

"He never misses," Lily whispered in amazement. She did not mean for the kangaroo to hear her words, but he did.

"I know," the kangaroo whispered back. "Like I told you in the forest, it's his beak. It's his secret weapon."

Ollie possessed an abnormally long beak for an ostrich, and when he bent down to shoot his marble with his wing, he would use his beak to line up his shot. He would extend his shooter marble out past the front of his beak and aim the marble, using his beak to sight in on his target.

When he let the marble fly from his wing, he didn't so much aim at the marble in the circle, but rather he concentrated his attention to the very point of his beak. Since his beak was very close to his eyes and therefore much easier to aim, Ollie's shot always flew arrow straight. He rarely missed knocking a marble out of the circle.

But the Kangaroo from Kookaburra was also a very good marble shooter, and he knocked one of Ollie's marbles out of the circle as the crowd applauded. Ollie then knocked Kangaroo's second marble out, and Kangaroo responded by knocking Ollie's second marble out of the circle. Ollie shot his third marble, as did Kangaroo, each knocking out one of their opponent's marbles. Ollie shot his fourth marble, and one of Kangaroo's marbles bounced from the circle. Kangaroo shot his fourth marble and watched it fly. The crowd erupted.

"He missed!" they shouted. "The Kangaroo from Kookaburra missed his marble!"

"Too bad, Kangaroo," the ostrich sneered. "But watch this."

Ollie moved up and sent his fifth shot flying. The crowd roared as the kangaroo's last marble flew from the circle. In the center of the circle now rested two of Ollie's marbles, for the Kangaroo from Kookaburra had missed on his fourth shot.

"You have only one shot remaining, Kangaroo," the Grand Master Walrus said, his voice a bit sad. "And you still have two marbles remaining within the circle."

"You'd better knock both of my marbles out with your next shot, Kangaroo," Ollie teased. "And getting two marbles out with one shot is impossible. You know that as well as me. Why don't you just give it up and go home?"

The Kangaroo from Kookaburra looked around at all the animals in the circle behind them. He feared Ollie the Ostrich was just about to beat him once more in front of the huge crowd. No one had ever knocked two marbles out of the circle with only one shot. It was unheard of in the world of marble shooting. Suddenly, Lily pulled the Kangaroo aside.

"You have to knock both marbles out with this shot," Lily said.

"I am sadly aware of that," the kangaroo said, shaking his head. "It just can't be done, Lily. I have never seen it done—ever."

173

"There's always a first time for everything," Lily assured him confidently. "I know how you can do it. There's got to be a way."

Then Lily explained her plan to him.

"Ollie uses his beak to aim his shooter marble," she said. "You need to use something too."

Then she pointed behind him.

"Kangaroo, why don't you use that long tail of yours?"

"My tail?" the kangaroo asked. "You want me to shoot my marble backward?"

"No, no," Lily explained. "Curl your tail up and let it hang over your head. When the tip of it dangles between your eyes, use it to line up Ollie's two marbles and then shoot hard. If your marble is straight and true, you can knock both of his marbles out with a hard shot."

"That sure sounds like a screwy idea," the kangaroo answered.

"Well, Ollie has used his beak to beat you five times in a row," Lily reminded him. "He certainly doesn't think that's such a screwy idea."

"But two marbles with one shot?" the kangaroo asked.

"You can do it," Lily assured him. "After all, weren't you the one who said you wanted to shut that old windbag ostrich up? Give it the old college try."

"Okay, I'll give it a try," the kangaroo said. "But I'm afraid I've never been to college either."

The kangaroo walked around the circle and stopped when he found the spot where Ollie's two marbles lined up. He curled his tail up and let it flop over his head where it dropped between his eyes. He heard snickering behind him but ignored it. As he lined up the marbles with the tip of his tail, the wind began to blow. His tail dropped to the ground.

"Oh, drat it!" he shouted. "Now my tail won't stay on my head!"

Lily looked around the circle and pondered her friend's dilemma. Then she walked over to Robert the Moose who, by coincidence, just arrived. She remembered her unfortunate incident a while back when her foot had become stuck in the moose's ear and how Einstein the Wise Old Owl had freed it with an unusual solution. Perhaps that solution would work again here. Lily climbed up the backside of the moose and scurried over to his ear.

"Excuse me, Robert," she said nonchalantly. "I need to borrow some of your earwax."

Before the startled moose could reply, Lily reached her paw inside the moose's ear and pulled a huge wad of gooey yellow wax. She hurried back down and ran over to the Kangaroo from Kookaburra. "Here," she said, showing him the large clump of moose wax. "We'll put this stuff on your head to hold your tail in place so you can shoot."

"Yuck and double yuck!" the Kangaroo exclaimed, making a face as he looked at the wad of yellow goo. "Do I really have to do this?"

"Do you want to win?" Lily demanded. "Do you want to shut that ostrich up for good?"

Lily turned her paw over and rubbed the earwax on top of the kangaroo's furry head. As she did, the kangaroo scrunched his shoulders toward his neck and made a face, for all this was rather disgusting to him. Then Lily placed the kangaroo's tail back on his head. The wind blew very hard, trying to knock the tail from its perch, but the tail was held firmly in place by the earwax. The Kangaroo from Kookaburra looked at Lily and grinned with a confidence Lily had not seen before now. Then he picked up his shooter marble and lined up Ollie's two marbles with the tip of his tail.

The kangaroo pushed his thumb hard against the finger holding his shooter marble and felt the pressure build in his thumb. As his thumb began to quiver, the Kangaroo from Kookaburra took a deep breath and closed his eyes. He heard a clunk as the pressure of his thumb launched the shooter marble into the circle faster than it had ever been shot before. The Kangaroo from Kookaburra watched in amazement as his shooter marble drove into Ollie's first marble and split it cleanly in half, sending the two halves flying from the circle. Without slowing a bit, the shooter marble drove toward Ollie's last marble and hit it squarely in the center, driving it from the circle and five feet into the grass.

At first the crowd surrounding the circle was silent, stunned by the incredible shot they just witnessed. Never before in the history of marble shooting had anyone ever shot two marbles out of the circle, let alone split one in half. And hitting a second marble so hard it landed five feet outside the circle is also just unheard of until now. The crowd began to cheer.

"We have a winner!" the Grand Master Walrus declared, grabbing the kangaroo's paw and raising it above his head. "Final shot wins it!"

Suddenly the crowd heard a loud squawking noise.

"Awk!" Ollie shouted. "Awk!"

You see, Lily snuck up behind the ostrich and plucked out Ollie's grandest tail feather sticking out a foot longer than all the others.

"I believe you owe me this," she grinned at Ollie as the ostrich rubbed his backside with a wing. "It will make a dandy quill pen! Ha-ha!" Lily tweaked one of the whisker hairs. "Too bad, ostrich. This would have made a fine toothpick."

Ollie's pride had been hurt in two ways, one much more painful than the other. But Lily thought the over-puffed bird had it coming.

Later that day, after the Kangaroo from Kookaburra had officially been declared the World Marble Shooting Tournament Champion, the crowd watched as the Grand Master Walrus opened the lock on the World Marble Shooting Tournament Goodie Bin and stepped back.

"Here, Kangaroo from Kookaburra," he smiled. "Get your forty-five pounds of goodies. Remember, whatever goodies you select are yours to keep."

The kangaroo entered the Goodie Bin and saw all the yummy goodies inside. He pulled out a cloth bag and began filling it with all sorts of things, mostly for his many friends back home. He gathered some eucalyptus leaves for his koala bear friends and some carrots for some hares living in what he called the Outback, even though he still considered them lowly creatures. The kangaroo also selected some coconuts and fresh grass for himself. After he'd stuffed forty pounds of goodies in his bag, he called to Lily.

"Lily," he said smiling, "for all the help and friendship you have given me, you may have my last five pounds of goodies. Go in and get whatever your little heart desires."

Now, I need not tell you that as fast as a jackrabbit can wink, Lily ran inside the Goodie Bin and grabbed five pounds of chocolate peanut clusters. She was quite happy with her goodies.

"I must go home now, Lily," the Kangaroo from Kookaburra said, "before all these goodies spoil. But I have one more thing for you."

The kangaroo took Lily's little paw and put something in it and then closed it with his own paw so Lily couldn't see what it was. Then he threw his cloth bag of treats over his shoulder and waved to all the animals. He began to walk away. He strode right past Ollie the Ostrich, who was still rubbing his backside where Lily had firmly plucked out the feather. When the kangaroo reached the edge of the Open Meadow, where the forest began, he turned and waved to Lily. As the kangaroo melted into the forest, with the click-click-click of marbles as his only companion, Lily turned her paw over to look at what her new friend had placed there.

A large shooter marble made of clear glass rested on her palm. Inside of the clear glass were brown swirls that seemed to be moving. And if someone were to stare closely at what was hidden within those swirls, one could slowly make out what appeared to be the head of the Kangaroo from Kookaburra, and across his face a beaming grin that spread from ear to ear.

CHAPTER 18

A PLACE IN THE HEART

It was a wonderful summer day in the Great Green Forest, with the weather so warm Lily crawled down from the safety of the trees to let her feet touch the cool soil of the forest floor. It was a different world down here. From high up in the trees, everything seemed smaller, and the squirrel could see all that was going on around her. But on the forest floor, her eyes could see only what was close by, for bushes and tall grasses prevented her from seeing any farther.

Lily headed down a narrow trail that was barely a trail at all. She knew right away mice and chipmunks, the only animals capable of navigating something so narrow, scurried over here often, for the path was well worn. In fact, Lily was forced to turn sideways on occasion so her body could fit between the bushes marking the edges of the trail. She continued down the path, her thoughts now on the warm batch of chocolate peanut clusters she had cooling on the big branch outside the door of her home in the Big Oak. She glanced up to the sky, admiring the clouds moving through the trees. It was a perfect day.

BOOM!

Lily suddenly found herself lying on her back, the result of some unknown force slamming into her and pinning her to the ground. She looked up to see stars spinning in front of her eyes, dancing and whirling in a blackness blocking out all other things. Her vision slowly began to clear, the stars sweeping away. She looked up and gasped. Pinning her to the ground were two strong paws. Above the paws the orange face of an animal she'd never seen before stared back at her. The animal's mouth was wide open, revealing sharp fangs, and behind them, a drooling pink tongue. The mouth spoke.

"Right on time, mouse. I knew if I waited long enough, breakfast would come to me. And here you are." Lily's body ached under the weight of this strange animal, and the pain, strangely enough, seemed to give courage to the squirrel.

"I am *not* a mouse!" she scolded in her bravest voice. "I'm a squirrel, if you must know. What kind of animal are you and what are you doing in the Great Green Forest?"

The expression on the animal's face turned from one of taunting to quizzical.

"What do you mean what am I?" the animal asked. "For heaven's sake, haven't you ever seen a cat before?"

"No, I've never seen a cat before, but I've heard of them," Lily shot back. "But this is a forest and cats don't live here. What are you doing here?"

The cat sneered. "Having breakfast, I hope." He pressed his paws down firmly on Lily's body. "And I can tell there's a lot of breakfast in you."

"Do cats eat squirrels?" she asked.

"Only when they have to," the cat replied. "I've never actually eaten one, but I haven't eaten in two days so I can't be choosy. Luckily, I found this trail and it smelled like mice so I staked it out. And then you came along."

"Well, I can assure you, cat," Lily said firmly, "I'm not what you want then. Now why don't you let me up and we can talk."

The cat drew its nose close to Lily.

"I don't know, squirrel," he sniffed. "You smell pretty sweet to me."

Suddenly Lily knew what the cat smelled on her that seemed to be sweet and good. "It's not me you're smelling at all, friend," she explained. "That's the food I intend to have for breakfast. I've just made a batch of chocolate peanut clusters and they're cooling right now. If you think the smell is wonderful, you should taste one. They're heavenly."

"Really," the cat answered with a tone of interest. "They sound intriguing."

"They are much more than just intriguing," Lily assured him. "And believe me, they're much tastier than any squirrel would be. Like I said, they're heavenly. And if you'd get your big paws off me, I can take you home and get you some."

The cat thought about Lily's offer for a moment and lifted his paws. He moved to one side, allowing Lily to rise from the ground. She stood up, wiping debris from her white fur.

"Well, that was fun," she said sarcastically. "Maybe next time you could hang me by my heels instead."

"Oh, stop, squirrel," the cat said. "I was only doing what my instincts told me to do and nothing more. It was nothing personal, you see."

"Looked pretty personal from where I was," Lily declared. "About as personal as one can get being so close to those fangs."

"Let's not quibble," the cat said. "After all, no one's been hurt." He stuck out his big orange paw, offering it to Lily. "My name is Dexter, anyway that's what my humans call me. I'm an orange tabby cat and very proud of it. Now who are you?"

"I'm Lily," she replied. "And I'm a squirrel, not a mouse, as I hope you've figured out."

Dexter paused, rubbing one paw over his chin. "Are you sure you're not mistaken? I've seen squirrels before, and they're brown or gray and they run all over the place. But none of them are white like you are."

Lily grabbed her tail and pushed it in front of her. "I can assure you I'm a squirrel. Does a mouse have a tail like this? Is a mouse this tall? No, I am definitely a squirrel."

"Well, why are you so white?" Dexter probed. "Aren't you sup-posed to be living up with the polar bears and artic foxes and hares? They're all white. You sure you're in the right place? Or are you some freak of nature?"

"I was born right here and I was raised right here in the Great Green Forest," she defended. "And I don't know why I'm white any more than you know why you are orange. But it is what it is and that's the truth of it. And by the way, what is a cat doing in the middle of a forest?"

"Good question," Dexter replied, looking around the forest. "Two days ago, I was quite content to be among my humans, especially the little one they call Mollie. She likes to pet me. Petting is something humans do to cats to make us purr. They run their hand across our back, and it makes our tail lift up and coaxes out loving sounds hidden deep inside of us. It makes them happy to do so, and I must say I like it as well. In fact, I have discovered if I purr very loudly, I get cat treats, and they are scrumptious. I'd much rather have a cat treat than a nasty old mouse any day."

"That doesn't sound like it would be a whole lot of fun," Lily answered. "I wouldn't want anybody messing with my fur, no matter what their good intentions happened to be."

"Well," Dexter offered, "let's just see about that."

The cat began stroking the squirrel, moving his paw up and down her back. Lily could feel a tingling where he rubbed, and soon the fur on her back stood straight up. Dexter noticed.

"See," he grinned. "I told you. You did everything I do but purr." He lowered his paw. "Now how about some of the breakfast you said was so good?"

"Okay," Lily answered. "But you still haven't told me how you happened to be in the Great Green Forest. You're the first cat, to my knowledge, who has ever come here."

"I'll explain it to you as we walk," Dexter said.

The two animals began moving along the path leading back to the Big Oak where Lily lived and where the chocolate peanut clusters sat cooling on the branch. A voice called out from high above.

"Hey, Lily," it said. "Where'd you find the pumpkin?"

Lily looked up to find Elvis the Toucan Bird.

"It's a little early for Halloween," Elvis added. "Nice of you to be planning ahead though."

"This is my friend Dexter," Lily shouted to him. "And he's a cat."

"I've heard about cats," Elvis answered. "I didn't know they'd be orange though."

"We're not all orange," Dexter cut in. "Some of us are black and some are white. Some are many colors. Most have short hair like mine, but others have long hair. There are lots of types. What kind of bird are you, by the way? I've never seen your kind before either."

"Why, I'm a toucan," Elvis replied proudly. "Ain't I magnificent to behold?"

"That's quite a yellow sniffer you've got sticking out in front of you," Dexter observed. "Why is it that you're not falling over from all that weight?"

"You just never mind," Elvis shot back. "That's my beak and it's light as a feather."

"Well, that's all wonderful, you guys," Lily interrupted. "But we must continue on. I've got something to show Dexter."

With that Elvis lifted his wings and flew away.

"How often does that bird get called Banana Nose behind his back?" Dexter asked.

"You're so bad," Lily chuckled, adding, "More often that he could ever imagine."

"Thought so," Dexter said.

Lily felt her eyes twinkling as she looked at the cat. Her fur tingled even though no one was petting her. *What was going on here?*

They soon arrived at the Big Oak, and to Lily's surprise, the big orange cat had no problem getting up the trunk of the tree. The cat, in fact, was quite adept at climbing. The chocolate peanut clusters had cooled and waited in rows to be tasted, which they did.

"Oh, my," Dexter said as he took the first bite. "These are quite delicious, Lily." He grinned at her. "I'm sure they taste much better than you would have."

"That's quite comforting to know," Lily answered, offering Dexter a second piece. "You can have another one if you tell me how you got here to the Great Green Forest."

Dexter took the second piece and munched on it.

"Fair enough," he said. "I was traveling with my humans on a train not far from here. My humans like to take me with them when they go to places. It seems I help little Mollie in ways I don't understand. She seems to get upset sometimes, and her parents pick me up and take me to her. Then she's not upset and goes to sleep. They call me her comfort cat. I always go where Mollie goes. Anyway, we were on a train and I was in a cage because that's the rule when we travel. Mollie must have thought I needed some air because it was a bit stuffy inside the rail car. While her parents slept, she took me outside in my cage and put me on a little platform just outside the door. There was a guard rail around this platform so humans wouldn't fall over, but as the train rounded a bend, Mollie lost her balance when the car jerked and accidentally kicked my cage, and over the side I went."

"That's awful!" Lily cried.

"Quite so," Dexter answered. "I heard Mollie calling out my name as I fell, but then I hit a steep bank and the cage slid down some grass a long way until it rammed into a tree. The door sprung open and I got tossed out. I ran back up the bank to catch the train but it was too late. The train sped down the tracks, and I was left alone, missing my Mollie. That was two days ago. I don't know how I'll ever find her, but for some reason, I sense she needs me." His eyes looked sad. "Quite a dilemma, don't you agree?"

Lily could offer no advice to the cat but did offer him some more peanut clusters. The cat ended up quite satisfied, eating half a dozen pieces. They had no further discussion about the little girl. The two sat on the branch, their stomachs full. The gentle rays of the sun piercing through the leaves warmed them, and soon they were both fast asleep on the branch of the Big Oak. When they awoke, the sun was beginning to set.

They awoke when something shook them. Lily's eyes opened to a wonderful sight, while Dexter's eyes woke to a horror. He shot up, his teeth bared, and his orange fur bristling. He backed away, his rear end pushing against the door of Lily's house.

"Egad!" he shouted. "What sort of a demon from the darkness is that!"

"Oh, Dexter," Lily laughed as she realized what had horrified the cat. "Some brave cat you are! That's just Mozart and he's my good friend."

"I've heard of such things," Dexter said in a tone of mistrust. "Sometimes things are mixed into food to fool the eater—is that what you did to me, Lily? Did you put something in those peanut clusters to make me see things that aren't there? Is this your idea of a joke?"

"Really, Dexter," Lily answered. "You need to just calm down." She put a paw on the little dragon's head. "You see, he's quite real, and he's just a tiny pink dragon who wouldn't hurt a flea. He's a special dragon who can do wonderful things."

"That's why I've come," Mozart explained. "I'm playing my Magical Mushroom Patch tonight in the clearing, and I wanted to make sure you came." Mozart shot a look over at the cat, now calmed down. "You can bring Mr. Orange Puss, if you'd like."

"His name is Dexter," Lily replied. "And he's just new to the forest."

"Well, Dexter," Mozart said. "You've picked a good day to be with us. I'm giving a concert tonight, and as a friend of Lily's, I extend you a heartfelt invitation to come."

Dexter looked over at Lily. "It'll be fun," she assured him. "Everyone will be there."

"Ok," Mozart said, raising his tiny dragon wings and lifting from the branch. "See you there." He drifted away into the waning daylight.

"What kind of place is this Great Green Forest I've stumbled into?" Dexter asked. "White squirrels, pink dragons, and a toucan with a banana beak—what else should I prepare my eyes to see?"

"There will be a few other surprises," Lily said, "both in sight and in sound. You'll find them all quite magical. But we'd better go or we'll be late."

Down from the tree they climbed, Lily once again leading as the pair headed to the clearing where the music was to be played. As they broke through the bush, they found the clearing was filled to the brim with forest animals. Robert the Moose was there, his antlers filled with birds, and next to Robert sat Freddie the Indian, looking dapper with an eagle feather jutting up from the back of his head and held in place with a thin red bandana. The two green bullfrogs, Finnegan and Finagle, sat on a rock at the edge of the clearing. Pine-Oak-E-O the Beaver sat whittling on a piece of wood with a shiny knife. Elvis the Toucan was there, his eyes surveying the crowd as he looked out over his long yellow beak. Einstein the Owl sat in a branch sagging under his weight as well as the weight of lots of other birds sitting next to him. As the smaller birds looked down, they spotted the orange furry creature among them and panicked.

"Cat! Cat!" they squawked. "A cat in the forest! Fly away! Fly away!"

A voice boomed over the squawking.

"Stop your infernal noise!" Einstein cried out. "Or you're going to upset everyone. We don't need a stampede here." He addressed Lily. "Is that cat with you, Lily?"

"Yes, Dexter is with me," she explained, pointing at the cat. "A strange misfortune has brought him into the Great Green Forest. He's not here to harm anyone. As you can see, he hasn't harmed me. He just wants to go home but doesn't know how to get there. He could use a few friends now, not a bunch of squawkers." She looked up at the birds and then around to all the animals of the forest. "How about it, forest friends? How about if we show this poor lost cat that kindness is alive and well in our Great Green Forest?"

"Very good words, Lily," Einstein agreed. He looked around. "Words we *all* should heed."

"Come, sit in front, Dexter!" Mozart yelled from the stage. "Come get close."

"What in the world is that?" Dexter asked as Lily and he approached the little dragon. "What is all that stuff?"

"Remember the magic I told you about?" Lily asked. "That here in the Great Green Forest magic is found both in sight and in sound? We have Mozart's Magical Mushroom Patch—and it is on those mushrooms Mozart plays his music. He is quite talented at playing." She winked at him. "You picked a great time to fall from a train."

"Funny," Dexter replied. "I wasn't aware there was a good time to fall from a train."

"Okay then," Einstein declared. "If we're through with all this demon cat foolishness, let us enjoy the evening's entertainment. Mozart, you can play for us now when you are ready."

"Suits me fine," Mozart replied, unflustered by what had just occurred. He began tapping lightly on the mushroom caps. "Just a little tuning," he explained to Dexter. "The moisture in the air affects their tone. This'll just take a second."

A few moments later, the little dragon was satisfied his drums were tuned and he began to play. The mushroom caps glowed as he tapped softly upon them. He began the concert as he always did, playing some music from his favorite composer, who happened to be named Mozart as well. The glowing notes rising from the mushroom caps drifted up into the night, delighting all who saw and heard them. Sparkling dust sprang from the mushroom caps as Mozart played and then floated back down.

A sense of calm passed over the crowd, and as it grew darker, the glow from the mushroom caps seemed to become brighter, and the floating notes above the clearing became a second sky. Mozart played more music—some classical, some jazz, some Celtic, and many other kinds. He even played music that made the crowd want to sing. Soon every forest animal was singing, and, from the trees, came the lovely sound of songbirds. Mozart suddenly stopped and looked toward Dexter.

"Perhaps, friends, since we have a guest with us this evening," he suggested, "we might ask him what song he wants to hear. What would you like to hear, Dexter, my good cat?"

"I don't think you'd know it," Dexter answered. "Too bad though— I'd love to hear you play it."

"I know a lot of songs," Mozart assured him. "What's the name of your song?"

"It's a song called 'What's New Pussycat,' and every cat in the world knows it by heart. But since there are no cats in your forest to teach you, how could you possibly know it?"

Lily turned to Dexter. "Remember that magic I was telling you about? Watch."

"I know that song!" Mozart declared.

"It's the magic," Lily whispered to Dexter.

"But if I'm going to play the music, I need someone to sing the words," Mozart explained. "So, friend Dexter, why don't you come up and help me out?" Mozart turned to the crowd. "What do you say, creatures of the forest! You ready to hear the cat yowl?"

The crowd roared their approval, and as Dexter jumped on stage, they roared even louder.

"Are you sure you know the words?" Mozart asked Dexter.

"Are you sure you know the music?" Dexter answered.

"Let's hit it then, shall we?" Mozart replied, raising his little dragon arms and tail over the glowing mushroom caps. "Start out fast and don't let the grass grow under your feet."

And that's just what happened. Mozart banged on the mushroom caps as Dexter stood straight up on his hind legs, gyrating his hips as he sang. Lily found the sight of the standing cat to be quite unsettling yet strangely satisfying as well, but she had no idea why. The music played very fast and the lyrics were very straightforward and interesting. The song posed a lot of questions about what this particular cat was doing and what was new in its life. Lily didn't understand why a cat would want flowers, as the song suggested it be given, or why a cat would ever want to powder its nose—that couldn't be good for sniffing at things and would clog up a smeller and make it useless for hunting. But Dexter went on and on with the song, and Lily couldn't help admiring this fine specimen of a cat. Dexter turned and stared right at her when he sang some words about somebody who would soon be kissing some sweet little pussycat lips which, for some reason, caused her to blush. Mozart banged away at the music as Dexter ended the song, singing about how he loved this pussycat's lips and eyes and nose, and Lily could only imagine what a special little pussycat she must have been to have a song written solely for her.

Lily slept lightly through the night, tossing and turning in her bed as Dexter slept on the branch of the Big Oak. She awoke early and cautiously slipped down the tree, careful not to wake the cat. She moved through the forest silently until she came upon the creature she had gotten up so early to find. He dozed comfortably in a tree, strange noises escaping from his owl beak as he dreamed.

"Einstein," Lily said in a soft voice that wouldn't awaken anyone sleeping nearby. "Wake up."

Lily called up to the owl several times, but he slept too deeply to hear her. Finally, she tossed an acorn and managed to hit him squarely between his eyes. He woke up immediately.

"How dare you!" he shouted, turning his head round and round. "Come out and fight, you scoundrel! Why, I'll—"

"Einstein," Lily spoke. "It's Lily. I'm down here."

The owl peered down, his eyes widening.

"Oh, yes, yes, Lily," he said. "You are up quite early, my dear. Are you not feeling well?"

"That's why I'm here," Lily answered. "To ask you about something. I don't know if I'm well or if I'm sick."

"What seems to be the problem, Lily?"

"I think I've caught something," she began. "I've never had these things happen before and I'm kind of scared."

"What kinds of things are you talking about?" the owl probed. "Tell me."

"I'm afraid I might die," she confessed. "My heart has been beating very fast lately, and my face feels flushed at times. It's a little scary, to be truthful about it."

"Have you been eating well?" Einstein asked. "Have you been getting enough sleep? Perhaps you're exercising too much." He poked a wing into his plump stomach. "I've never had such a problem, as you can see."

"None of those," she said quickly. "That I know. But I fear it's something very bad, and I know where it came from."

"Go on," urged the owl. "Tell me."

Lily glanced around, afraid of being heard. "I am afraid I have caught some affliction from Dexter, the cat you met last night, and I feel quite ashamed. For if I have caught it, so will all those who attended the concert last night. We are all doomed if that is the case."

"That sounds reasonable," the owl said. "But let's not panic just yet." He thought for a moment. "Let's think here—your heart is racing and your body is hot. When does this occur and how often?"

"Well," Lily began. "This never used to happen at all, but just when Dexter arrived. He brought this affliction with him. I'm sure of it."

"Just one question then, Lily," the owl answered. "Does Dexter have the same symptoms?"

"Well, no," Lily answered in a surprised tone, as if something just dawned on her. "No, he doesn't appear to anyway."

"You've spent a lot of time with him lately," Einstein added. "I think you'd know if he had some illness."

"Well, what is it then?" Lily asked. "What's going on here?"

"How'd you sleep last night?" the owl asked.

"Terribly," Lily shot back. "Just terribly."

"And why was that, Lily?"

"Bad dreams I suppose," was her reply.

"What kind of dreams?" the owl probed.

"I can't rightly recall," she answered. Then, like a bolt of lightning out of the blue, her dream appeared to her.

"No!" she screamed. "No, we didn't!"

"What is it, Lily?" the owl demanded. "What was in the dream?"

"Noses," Lily said somewhat dazed by her revelation. "We were rubbing noses in my dream. Dexter and I were on the branch of the Big Oak, rubbing noses, of all things." She looked up at the owl as if ashamed and then hesitated a moment before continuing. "And I'm afraid I quite liked it."

Einstein stared down at the squirrel and roared with laughter, his body shaking so hard feathers dropped from his body and floated to the ground.

"You've got an affliction all right, girlfriend," he chuckled. "You've got a crush on a cat, is what you have."

Lily thought back to the instant she had met Dexter and how he intended for her to be his breakfast. But they had ended up becoming friends and sharing much in the little time they spent together. The cat had been very nice to her, and she enjoyed being with him. But Dexter also made it clear he needed to get back to Mollie who, for some reason, badly needed him near her.

"Oh, Einstein," she moaned. "You mustn't tell him—not ever. He must never know of this."

She went on to explain how the cat came to be in the forest and how he longed to get back to Mollie and how she needed him to give her comfort.

"I know how I feel about my friend Dexter," she confessed to the owl. "If I feel this way about him after so short a time, just imagine how Mollie feels after having him close for such a long time. We must help him. We must help Dexter find Mollie and get them back together."

"You are correct, Lily," the owl agreed. He thought for a moment. "Trains—that's what we need to do. Find the train and find when the trains come through. I bet your Mollie will be on one of those trains, looking for her cat."

"We've got to find her fast," Lily said with urgency in her voice. "Dexter says she needs him. Oh, what tragedy will befall Mollie if we fail to find her!"

"You need to go to Dexter and tell him of our plan," Einstein directed. "You must prepare him for what is to come." He pointed a wing toward the Big Oak. "Go quickly. I have an urgent matter to which I must attend."

Lily rushed to the Big Oak and woke up Dexter. She told him of their idea to help find Mollie so the cat could give comfort to the little girl. She explained to him Einstein was working on a plan and would reveal it later, which is exactly what the owl did.

"I found the cage," Einstein explained. "It's right next to the railroad tracks, at the bottom of a grassy slope."

"As it should be," Dexter agreed, grinning with satisfaction. "That's right where I left it."

"Then we know what to do," Einstein continued. "We go to the cage and wait. That's our only hope. Mollie must have known where the cage fell, and hopefully she will be back with her humans. Then Dexter can go back to her."

Dexter stared over at Lily, a quiet sadness in his eyes.

"Yes," he said. "That is what we must do. Mollie needs me."

"How do we know she will even come back?" Elvis the Toucan suddenly asked. The bird landed in a nearby tree a short time earlier and had been listening to the plan. "Maybe this Mollie has found another cat."

"Nothing like having an optimist among us," Einstein said sarcastically to Elvis. "You're just a peach of a bird, aren't you? Or perhaps I should say banana."

"Just keeping it real," the toucan answered, running a wing across the top of his yellow beak. "And I've heard all the Banana Nose cracks already, thank you."

"My sources tell me there are two trains a day along that track that carry passengers," Einstein continued. "Just two is all. Knowing this will simplify things."

"Maybe she's already come and gone," Elvis speculated. "Did you ever think about that?"

"I have," Einstein answered. "But that's a possibility we will have to deal with. The only way we will truly know is to wait for the train to come by."

Which is exactly what they did. Einstein and Lily traveled with Dexter to the spot where Einstein located the cage that had once held the cat. There were two trains the first day, neither of which even slowed when nearing the bend from where the cage had tumbled. On the second day, the early train sped by and merely blew its whistle. As they waited, Lily and Dexter continued to stay together, enjoying moments they both knew might soon become just pleasant memories.

"Wait!" Einstein shouted, his sharp sense of hearing alert. "I hear the second train! It's coming!"

A whistle pierced the silence, and they could all hear the sound of the approaching train. The sound grew closer and the railroad tracks shook.

"It's slowing down!" Dexter shouted. "Look! It's slowing down!"

As the engine rounded the bend, the train slowed but did not stop.

"Hey!" Lily shouted. "Stop! Stop! Please stop!"

Half of the cars passed them when, as if by some magic borrowed from the Great Green Forest, the train screeched to a halt. The train sat silently on the tracks as if it were some great beast waiting to be stirred from its slumber, clouds of steam pouring from beneath the engine. Suddenly a door opened on the end of one of the rail cars sitting right in front of the group. To their surprise, out stepped a tall, lanky man wearing a suit coat and top hat. The man was vaguely familiar to Lily, and she searched her mind to find an answer. As she was just about to give up, the man removed his hat, and what looked like a mountain of black hair fell like a landslide over his shoulders. Lily knew who the man was now. There could be no mistake. He was Freddie the Indian. Freddie waved at them from the platform as if he expected them to be there.

"What in the world are you doing here, Freddie?" Lily asked in total amazement. "Are you lost or something?"

"No," the Indian replied, smiling. "I'm not the one who's lost. I'm an Indian and we always know where we are." He turned toward the door and curled his finger, motioning for someone to come out. A young girl appeared on the platform. Freddie addressed Einstein. "You were right, Einstein, as usual. I found them at the train depot and brought them here."

The girl squealed when she spotted Dexter.

"My cat!" she shouted. "My cat! Dexter! Dexter, come here!"

Dexter shot off toward the girl as tears filled her eyes. The cat hurled himself into her arms and she hugged him tightly, sobbing with joy. From the door of the train emerged a man and a woman. The man spoke to Freddie.

"I can't thank you enough, friend," he said. "I don't know how you knew about all of this, but we are grateful you knew and could help us. Mollie needs this cat, and I mean for more than just a pet. It means the world to her to have him back."

Freddie looked at the girl hugging the cat. "My work here is done. I will go now."

As the stunned couple watched, wondering why anyone would want to leave a train in the middle of nowhere, Freddie climbed over the platform rail and slid down the bank. Freddie motioned to the train conductor to go.

"Wait!" Lily shouted, bounding up the bank. She launched her white body onto the platform and looked at the little girl and then to Dexter. The girl, sensing something was going on, bent over and eased the cat down toward the squirrel.

"I'm going to miss you, Dexter," Lily said through blurry eyes.

"And I am going to miss you, Lily," Dexter replied as a tear formed in his eye. "You are quite a squirrel."

Then, for reasons known only to Mother Nature, the two animals gently rubbed their noses together. The train lurched and Lily knew it was time to go.

"Don't forget me, Dexter," Lily said

"How could I ever forget you, Lily?" Dexter answered. Lily turned and leapt from the platform as the train pulled away. Einstein and Freddie were waiting for her at the bottom of the hill, waving to the departing train. Lily looked up at Freddie.

"You're looking pretty human in that outfit, Chief," she teased.

"Well, don't hold it against me," Freddie replied. "It won't happen again, I can promise you that."

With that the Indian took off his suit, leaving him wearing only the loincloth he usually wore. He walked into the Great Green Forest, tossing the clothing and top hat into some bushes. He returned to his friends.

"Why do humans bother to wear all these things?" he asked, shrugging his shoulders. "They're such a hassle."

"I guess we'll never know," Einstein said with a wide sweep of a wing. "You know these humans." He looked around. "But it's time to go. It is quite a journey back home."

So off they went, making their way back to the safety of the Great Green Forest. Lily found the trail to the Big Oak, her nose tingling with excitement for many days afterward as the memory of that moment with Dexter when they touched noses flooded her dreams. Lily knew that, in the weeks and months to follow, she and her friends in the Great Green Forest would partake in many great adventures and make all sorts of new friends along the way. And Lily looked forward to it all.

CPSIA information can be obtained
at www.ICGtesting.com
Printed in the USA
JSHW041500040522
25542JS00005B/67